Universal Talk Laws

How to Increase Your Net Worth with Words

Kinja Dixon

Author, Speaker, Consultant

Cover Art by Phu Nguyen, CEO Phusion PC
Edited by Kimberly T. Matthews

ISBN: 978-0-615-88017-4

FOR INFORMATION CONTACT:
Kinja Dixon: kdixon@kinjadixon.com
Please visit online at www.kinjadixon.com

Online ordering is available for all products.
Website Design by Manselle Media

Table of Contents

Acknowledgements 5

Preface. 11

Introduction 14

Chapter 1: When Opportunity Knocks,
            You Have to Open the Door 19

Chapter 2: Before the Light Bulb Turned On 24

Chapter 3: What is Your Purpose? 31

Chapter 4: Mindset 36

Chapter 5: The Science of Selling. 45

Chapter 6: The Mindset of the Customer 50

Chapter 7: How to Start Your Day as a
            UNIVERSAL Talker 58

Chapter 8: Greeting. 64

Chapter 9: The Discovery. 72

Chapter 10: Company Credibility 78

Chapter 11: The Recommendation Phase 82

Chapter 12: The Closing of the Sale 88

Chapter 13: Successful Living Comes With Commitment . 96

Highlights from UNIVERSAL TALK LAWS 100

For further self-development I recommend. 102

More Acknowledgments 103

Acknowledgements

*No one gets to where they are without help in
some form from others, and the quicker you forget
who assisted you in your journey, the further
you will remain from your full potential. KD*

ach day is a gift and you should be eager to open your daily present. As I reflect on the chain of events that brought me to this point in my life, writing a book, I do realize that every action and reaction played a role in this development. I want to thank Life for all that it has given, and it is only fitting that I give special acknowledgements to certain people who assisted me along my journey.

I thank my mother, Edna Dixon-Lawson. She grew up in North Carolina, but made a life-altering decision in August, 1970. After graduating from Lenoir Community College in Kinston, North Carolina, she relocated to Brooklyn, New York where she felt she would have a better chance of getting a career started in her field of study, and more opportunities for advancement.

She met my father, Leroy Mcclarin in 1975; I was born on December 14, 1978. Subsequently, I did not grow up in a traditional two-parent household because my parents did not marry. However, in my particular situation, I feel that this scenario did not adversely affect me because both families were supportive of all stages of my development. When I think back, I realize that my mother made positive decisions that added to my ability to succeed in life. I am so very thankful for her literally giving everything she had to ensure that I became a success. I am a primary example that if you give your all as a parent great things will happen. It truly takes a village to raise a child. The foundation she gave to me through constant development and concern for my future allowed every successful moment from the time of my birth forward to come to fruition.

I thank my father, who always played a part in my world. When I was fifteen, he and my step-mom, Earlene gave me a mental wake-up call. At a time when I thought I knew everything, they helped prepare me for the harsh realities of the real world. I know that I do tell him enough, but I sincerely thank him for his involvement and influence that contributed to my growth. There would be no me without him.

I want to thank my Godmother, Helen Murphy, and her mother - my Grandma, Ms. Maude, who would never let me go outside to play in the streets of Brooklyn. I spent time with them occasionally after school and they ensured that I was fully protected when I was in their care. Today, as an adult, I thank them for their over protection. I was safe because of it.

I would like to thank the principal and teachers of Arista Prep Academy in Brooklyn. This was the private school where many valuable lessons were instilled in me and are still useful to this day. From first to sixth grade, I wore that burgundy and gray uniform. I will always appreciate the curriculum of that school.

I thank the faculty and staff of Paul Robeson High School in Brooklyn for preparing me for the adult life, and a special thanks to the class of 1996 who voted me "Most Popular" and "Class Clown" during my senior year. That was really an honor to a 17-year-old. At least once a year, I glance at my yearbook and reflect on my high school days.

I thank my Aunt Linda and Uncle Curt. I spent several weeks with them before going into the U. S. Air Force. My Uncle Curt was a military veteran and helped prepare me mentally with the guidance and strict discipline I needed; he prepared me physically with the schedule and routine workout which gave me an idea of how military life would be. My transition would not have been as smooth without the two of them providing significant guidance at such a critical time in my growth and development.

I thank the leaders in the U. S. Air Force and all of our other armed forces for (1) helping to protect this land of opportunity and (2) for opening my eyes to another world outside of Brooklyn, New York. That structured method of training introduced during boot camp still helps me stay focused to this day. My occupational skill was an aircraft structural mechanic. I still remember painting an airplane for the first time.

I thank Davino Richardson, a very close friend who called and told me about the telemarketing opportunity he was taking advantage of at the time after my transition out of the military. Without the entry into the communication field I would not possess and be able to share the insight you are now reading.

My telemarketing position ended due to a company site shutdown in 2004, which led me to Wyndham Vacation Ownership. I truly thank this company for providing the opportunity which has helped immensely to turn me into the person that I have become today. I did not start off well at all, and I thank Brendon and Tara Dow, the two mentors who played a key role in helping me push forward at a very uncertain time in my life. One conversation with Brendon during my third month of sales inspired a life change that led to a consistently successful career afterward.

In 2009 the site in Williamsburg, Virginia introduced a new Vice President, Butch Gunter. This man has taught me so much in the time that he has been in my world. His college football background and tremendous range of knowledge in several areas helped his attention to detail and methods of instilling desire to the masses. I would also like to thank him for submitting my performance accomplishments to be judged independently by the Stevie and ARDA foundations in 2012, and I am deeply appreciative of his support throughout my career.

I thank Barbara Henderson, who was my manager at Wyndham from 2009 until her retirement in June 2013, and now travels the world with her husband. She taught me one of the most valuable lessons that I will never forget, and I am humbly appreciative of it. Barbara told me that one of the keys to continuous success is to learn how to build businesses from the ground up and sell them off if you need to. Those are simple words, yet when that method of thinking is built upon, you become much more successful. Of the four types of earners described in *Rich Dad Poor Dad* by Robert Kiyosaki, Barbara is definitely an investor and business owner.

I am extremely thankful for the year of 2009. It was a very pivotal year in my growth for several reasons, but mainly because it was the year that my mother found out she had breast cancer. Due to the research and procedures that she underwent, it was removed. I thank the doctors and scientists who dedicate their lives to helping eliminate the health issues that come with diseases of all kinds. Using the principles I learned from a life changing read that I highly recommend, Napoleon Hill's, *Think and Grow Rich*, I researched my family's background and decided to change my life at that time as well.

During that phase of my life I weighed 305 pounds, with thirty-five percent body fat. I sought help from a nutritionist and bodybuilder, Carl Frady, III, who helped me change my life in a major way. I dropped seventy-five pounds and twenty-two percent body fat within a year under his guidance. As I write this book, I weigh in at 195 with seven percent body fat. The disciplines that I gained through changing my daily habits definitely contributed to my overall success. Thanks Carl.

I am thankful for my two most recent relationships in the last three years which have had a major part in my personal growth as a man, and also contributed to all of my life movements.

The young lady I dated from 2009 until 2011, when she was accepted into a government contract in Africa, helped teach me how to communicate more effectively when in a relationship. One of the books we read together was *The 5 Love Languages* by Gary Chapman. I truly value and recommend it to anyone currently married or planning to ever get married.

My most recent relationship ended because our growth took us in different directions. This relationship taught me several lessons. The most valuable principle that I took away was that all pain can be turned into positive production. This book is a product and direct reflection of what can be done if you positively channel your feelings in the right direction when you plan for something but it does not end up how you intended.

I thank my close friend and business partner, Robert Cuff, III, who shared so many ideas with me that helped expose the creative side of my brain. The business idea he shared with me on our first plane ride from Dominican Republic was a true eye opener. I have many more places to see in the world, however, the ancient ruins in Mexico, Panama Canal, getting one of the best haircuts that I ever received in the inner cities of Dominican Republic, and learning how to ride a scooter in the Bahamas have been taken off of my to-do-list.

I also thank Xavier Bryan, whom I have known for several years. He has taught me many lessons that have heavily contributed to the path that I am now on. He has helped me understand the true meaning of freedom. One of his personal goals was to put himself in a position where he could satisfy his financial goals, maintain the freedom to be a better husband to his wife, and to devote more time to develop his daughter. I saw him attain each of his personal goals with my own eyes within a matter of months. When he shared his thoughts about time and how most people relate it to money, I was inspired forever. Time cannot be paid back.

The places I frequented, the events I attended, situations encountered, and the challenges I confronted and overcame, were instrumental in the choices I made, choices that were directly influenced by the above mentioned individuals. I would have made different decisions had it not been for my interaction with them.

I also thank the numerous authors that have written books concerning self-development, life management, and success principles. I have listed some of those titles in the back of this book. I would not have the insight that I gained so early in my life without becoming a student on a daily basis. I would like to thank Life again for giving me any obstacles, troubles, and pain that I have had to overcome. Once you realize that all adversity strengthens your character, you train yourself to turn all troubles into triumph.

PREFACE

First and foremost I would like to thank the Creator for allowing life for all, because without life nothing would exist. I want to thank the Stevie Awards, which recognize achievements for sales, customer service, call center and business development professionals worldwide. I also thank the American Resort Development Association (ARDA), a Washington DC trade association that represents resort development and vacation ownership industries worldwide. Between these two organizations, thousands of established companies very well known for customer satisfaction are judged annually for excellence in several categories such as new products and services, solution providers, advertising, and volunteer of the year to name a few.

With any how-to-book, credibility is of the utmost importance. Based on my 2012 sales performance, I achieved the honor of winning the Gold Stevie Award for Sales Representative of the Year in All Other Industries (industries excluded were computer software and hardware), in all the world on February 25, 2013 at the Paris Hotel and Casino in Las Vegas, Nevada. The honor of the American Resort Development Association Award for the Top Salesperson for In-house Sales for vacation ownership, again in the world, was presented to me on April 10, 2013 at the Westin Diplomat Resort in Hollywood, Florida.

During approximately nine years of a very successful career with

Wyndham Vacation Ownership, financially setting myself and my family up for life, I earned the freedom to explore my inner thoughts more carefully. The skill set required to achieve these honors did not just happen overnight. I am thankful for the continuous self-development which helped me to attain my consistently increasing performance in what some call the toughest sales industry in the world. I am also thankful that I witnessed a company restructuring plan after the 2008 economic crash that had Wyndham Worldwide (WYN), the parent company of Wyndham Vacation Ownership take its stock from $4 to over $50 per share. This achievement ranked Wyndham Worldwide as the biggest winner of the top performing components of the S&P 500 from March 2009 to March 2012, experiencing an increase of more than 1311% according to Forbes magazine. My ability to continue to succeed with the company after 2008 was mainly due to the execution of that plan. The wisdom gained from watching it happen from the inside out was priceless.

Throughout my career I have helped innumerable people, but my scope was broadened because of the history and significance of these two organizations recognizing my performance. There were more than one million representatives competing all over the world, so when I achieved the honors, I was instantly inspired and felt obligated to do more.

At both recognition events I met people from all over the world who set the standard for excellence in sales and customer service. I was truly honored to be in the presence of such greatness. I thought, what about the salespeople who are not here but would like to increase their performance to allow their time at the office to be used more effectively? How can I assist the millions of people who are not in a direct sales position but want to further their employment/ life ranking by learning persuasion methods? What is a quick, yet effective way to get this information out to the individuals all over the world who need it and would apply it to their daily lives? After much prayer, the voice in my head, my inner spirit, insisted that I follow my heart. Consequently, the thought of a handbook came to mind: a handbook designed to help increase self-production in all people.

My main objective is for you to benefit from my growth.

Introduction

*Enjoy each moment of your victory as you
continuously enhance your definition of
what it is to truly win. KD*

Congratulations for taking this step toward improving your persuasion techniques by reading *UNIVERSAL TALK LAWS*. The title refers to a guidance based system that allows you to increase production in life advancement, communication, and sales universally. They are all more related than you may have thought which is why this information will greatly bring an alignment to your view of life. How you talk to yourself determines how you talk to others and your results in life are a direct reflection of those conversations.

This may be one of the most impactful advanced communication/life books that you will ever read. My goal was to simplify the process of how the universal laws work with experience based direction, versus confusing propaganda based off of theory. I know your time is valuable and that is why I wrote this to ensure you make the most of it, in and out of the office. When your heart is in the right place and the strategy that you use has been proven as successful, you will always deliver great results. This is an easy-to-read guide that will immediately increase your productivity in person-to-person communication. This was written so that you can experience long term life growth, but in a form that allows you to refer to it during certain parts of your sales process for an instant impact in your daily routine as well. It will also take a closer look into the mind of an average person from very humble beginnings that created, and then followed proven success methods which influenced his way of living in a very dramatic way.

My main schooling was conveyed through more than 26,000 hours so far of aggressive practice in a very successful sales career which I am so grateful to have experienced. During my learning process, I kept documentation and created step-by-step personal achievement formulas that have helped me consistently and effectively communicate to individuals of all ages, races and genders, even with varied attitude and behavior patterns. What makes this so much more valuable for you is that during my years of self-development, I implemented the lessons of masters: Napoleon Hill, Dale Carnegie, Brian Tracy, Zig Ziglar, Les Brown, Darren Hardy, Jim Rohn, Anthony Robbins, and Robert Kiyosaki just to name a few. My internal desire to win was heavily inspired by these leaders which play a big part in my solid foundation. When I combined their philosophies for success with my communication approach, a window of opportunity was opened for my name to be placed in the history books of outstanding sales performances. You will understand why I am so confident that you will change your life for the better if you commit to and apply the laws presented in this book.

You are on your way to gain from all that I know which will strengthen your current expertise. This will benefit you whether you are talking face to face or over the phone, closing $10 deals or

$500,000 deals, at the worst of your game or trying to take your skill to another level. You will gain by learning principles rather than simply opinions. As Abraham Lincoln quoted, "People will pass away but principles never will. Principles live forever." Therefore, in this work, I am giving you everything that I have learned thus far about how to communicate to yourself and to others while increasing your net worth. I will share with you:

- The steps to being able to speak to anyone at any time and produce desired results
- The development of a mental roadmap
- How to improve performance in all tasks
- Ways to get quicker promotions within your company
- Easier persuasion methods to use with anyone about anything
- How to increase your overall mental stability

Getting where you want to be in life depends on knowing how to universally talk through all situations. This is a book written by a twelve-year veteran in face-to-face sales. However, applying these principles will assist anyone who communicates with others regardless of position, occupation or career field. I would like everyone to acquire and apply this wisdom with integrity to benefit those who you do business or interact with, not to take advantage of them. I emphasize this point because the average person does not realize that there are scientifically proven methods that are used in getting individuals and masses to move in certain ways.

My entire mindset was not based on taking the easy way out. That route would have had me solely set another personal performance goal for myself and meet it like I have done repeatedly for over a decade. We are all born to inspire in one way or another and I am grateful that I have a platform to deliver my testimony. I am a true believer that the more you help mankind while providing a service, the better servant to the world you become. It is now time that you benefit from my previous struggles and save yourself time which you cannot get back. The more you are able to take away from this work now, the more you can reap immediate benefits from this insight beginning today.

This book will deliver the best results only if you realize you have untapped potential that you would like to be released. There is no one magic sentence, and I expect you to challenge my thoughts, but at least consider them. This book will give you all that you put into it once you decide to make success a lifestyle instead of a special event. When I decided to change my lifestyle and go from 305 pounds to the 195 pounds that I am today, I had to commit to the success patterns and you will have to do the same with this information in regards to the results you expect to receive. Do not be the only person in your circle to read this and not reap the reward that is in it for you because of being set in your ways. Be willing to challenge any bad habits that are uncovered to replace them with good ones. I promise that if you apply the techniques presented in this book and fully commit to the Universal Talk Laws, you will produce better results in all that you do, regardless of whether you sell for a living or not. That is a bold statement that I am very confident in stating publicly and with certainty.

At the end of each chapter, there is a summary that highlights the lessons expressed in each chapter of my growth. The first two chapters are very important because they detail the initial steps of my highway of life which led to roadblocks that almost stopped my success from coming to fruition. Unfortunately, the majority of people do not overcome obstacles in their life because their obstacles are not viewed as stepping stones. To help create a personal road map for your success, make note of any additional insight you have gained through your perception. This will give you a personalized manual that can be used as a reference with your Universal Talk Law Guide as you continue or begin dominating in all that you do starting today. You have some very powerful information in your grasp that will change your life and the life of anyone you choose to share it with. In that vein, please pass any knowledge you acquire to someone else to play your part in the process.

Chapter 1

When Opportunity Knocks, You Have to Open the Door

Every ending creates a new beginning.
It is totally up to you where that start will finish. KD

I f I had not been introduced to the sales industry in the year 2000, I would not have had the experiences that led to this path of my journey. It was in this industry where I came to realize the importance and impact of effective communication. The sales profession is usually not on the list of careers that a child would choose and plan to do when he or she grew up. My arrival into sales was not planned, but it has truly been a blessing for which I am very thankful.

My first move as a civilian after leaving my tour of duty with the Air Force at Langley Air Force Base in Virginia was to secure employment with a home builder that specialized in custom homes in the Ford's Colony area of Williamsburg, Virginia. I enjoyed it so much that within a year of working with the company, I became one of the leaders of the crew making $500 a week.

One day a friend of mine, Davino, whom I'd known for about a year, called me and said, "I just got a check for almost $1000 in a week from talking on the phone!"

After some research, I found out about a weekend shift at the telemarketing company where Davino worked. I considered the point that a weekend-shift would allow me to test out an alternate earning opportunity while I continued my full-time carpentry position, so I decided to do exactly that. The Saturday and Sunday schedule grossed me the same pay that I made for a whole week's work with the builders! I was 21 years of age with the hunger for more so I decided to make it a full-time position. The rest is history. Davino's one call led to so much more than I could have ever expected.

Within six months, I became a manager and experienced at that time, the four most financially profitable years of my life. My interest in the art of selling grew and my view of life was forever transformed.

In the managerial role with that company, eighty percent of my weekly income was derived from managing a team of fourteen to twenty-one people on a weekend shift. Most of my representatives had a part-time mentality to sell phone service, and I was going to "go broke" or push myself to extraordinary limits. Their performance was a reflection of my leadership which meant I had to instill my performance beliefs into them quickly to ensure we could all benefit. When I studied how to motivate a team, I learned that being able to properly communicate was a similar trait in all successful people. Role playing was one of the most effective ways to help my team communicate better and our results were heavily impacted, which caused everyone to be more content with the results. Many more customers received lower phone bills because of the new plan they signed up for, my representatives received higher pay with more confidence in their daily interactions and I felt great for helping to change lives so early in my career.

The traits instilled into my team forced them to deprogram the "coast by to get a buck" mindset. With that mentality gone, the team was then able to start separating themselves from the pack because excellent performance became our standard. Looking back, I see that this was relevant to my personal growth for which I am grateful. Persistence, confidence, and striving for perfection can be developed in any position, but in a performance based career, certain attributes are mandatory to perform at a high level consistently. One of the biggest challenges that I finally helped my team overcome was to never let rejection discourage their future optimism. Each minute brings a new opportunity.

Life was good. My yearly income was over $70,000 a year and according to the average household's income I considered myself to be in a great, financially secure position. I enjoyed going on special company trips and attending recognition events for performance-based competitions. I will say that it was a life that I had really gotten used to. One of the best feelings I experienced was looking at college kids come in for part-time jobs, graduate, and leave more prepared for the real world with the knowledge I contributed through my guidance and expertise to their life journey. I was very comfortable and planned on making this my career. Everything was going great. Then in the summer of 2004, due to decisions by the President and CEO of the company, we found out that the entire site was closing down. Once again my life took another turn.

At twenty-five years old, after thinking I had a solid career, I discovered, with harsh reality, that nothing is ever guaranteed. Several lessons were taught which prompted me to take a longer look down this road called life. Always expect the unexpected was one lesson and staying on top of current events in regards to the industry you work in was another that immediately stuck with me.

The sudden fear of being dependent on any company to secure my future caused me to start educating myself on the other ways that people managed their financial portfolios. Robert Kiyosaki's *Rich Dad Poor Dad* helped introduce me to the information I needed. You must educate yourself on ways to make your money grow no matter how much you earn annually. I realized due to financial pressures on myself, I needed to seek higher education on how to create bigger steps toward wealth by becoming a much better manager of my yearly income. That book showed me that there are four types of earners in this world: Employees, Self Employed, Investors and Business Owners. The fact that almost all investors and business owners started off as employees really made me do some self-reflection. I had no major investments at that time, and I did not have an exact business in mind but I figured that it would not hurt to at least start learning the traits that could one day help me go further into that direction. I also wondered why my main goal was strictly set to work for someone else, instead of myself. It all had to do with how I communicated to myself, the executive director of my life's movie. No matter what you do for a living, you should manage your daily duties as if it is your own business and one day it just might be.

A recruiter in the area contacted me with good news; Fairfield Resorts (now Wyndham Vacation Ownership), had immediate employment opportunities available. This was and still remains the largest vacation ownership company in the world. I was very excited, to have been told about the opportunity, and to become a part of this model organization. The transition from working on planes and homes to managing representatives, to talking about the benefits of a vacation ownership seemed awkward, however, embracing change is what I call it when I look back on that phase of my life.

Vacation ownership was an entirely different beast in every aspect. Wyndham Vacation Ownership taught me how to turn challenge into championship and create vacation memories for millions.

SUMMARY   You have learned that each opportunity afforded to you has a reason. You are clear that the characteristics needed to perform at a high level in a commission based employment opportunity are the same characteristics needed to be successful in life. You have learned that even though you should never expect the worst, the more you educate yourself during your good times, the better off you will be during any challenges you may face.

Chapter 2

Before the
Light Bulb Turned On

Your reality is only based upon what you
have seen through your eyes. You will continue
to overlook the opportunities to change your
way of living until your view gets clearer. KD

"When did the light bulb turn on?"

Over the years, I have been asked that question about my sales career from my co-workers, family, friends and associates. My answer will explain what led me down the path of the light bulb almost not turning on at all. It is my hope that my experience helps in your pursuit of freedom, because walking away from a blessing before it fully blossoms can ultimately slow down your process.

Life is no fairy tale and for you to fully get the effect of this tutorial, I have to be completely honest about how I almost ran away from my light.

It was March 2005. I was in my third month of Member Services in vacation ownership with Wyndham and I was in a very unproductive state. My job included helping owners learn about their account, however, I did not completely understand the product system, and Wyndham's extensive training program was not the problem. Several people from my training class seemed to catch on fairly quickly. I have to admit that I comprehended at a slower pace due to my daily reflections.

I had felt secure at my previous job but my length of service plus hard work and dedication were repaid by being told that the entire site was shutting down. Imagine being called into an emergency meeting and told in July that you would be unemployed in November. Four Months! Of course that was an ample amount of time to prepare for a new opportunity, which I did, but I was very angry at the uncertainty brought into my world. When I left the telemarketing company in 2004, I was not mentally prepared for what my future would hold. Up until that point in my life I never experienced those feelings before.

I'd never let go of my resentment over the company's downsizing, and found a new position without proper mental preparation. I had no real desire to learn the process to get the results my employer desired and I let the wrong emotions take control. This was all taking place during a transition time in my life. One thousand dollars was being deducted from my savings account to pay bills every month. Fear started to set in about how long I could continue to have monthly deductions without making deposits. My thoughts about life were far from optimistic, which attributed to my short temper. I drove 30 minutes to and from work every single day, wondering why I was even wasting my time. Consequently, I just kept waking up and repeating the same process over and over again with the hopes of future success. What I did before was so much easier in comparison and I just wished life had not become so complicated.

It was getting close to the end of month three and I had to start weighing my options. I had my certification but did not want to go back into the aircraft mechanic world. Going back to being a carpenter was not on the top of my list either; I had to do something.

I got a call from an associate of mine, a previous co-worker that transferred within the company that I was laid off from. He had moved to Maryland and was calling to tell me that they needed managers, and due to my previous management experience they were very interested in interviewing me. I did some research and even drove to Maryland during my following days off to look at the facility and apartments in the area. I was pleased with what I saw, and felt my sense of security coming back because there was a base salary plus commission for the position. I made a decision to relocate.

The next step was to give Fairfield Resorts a two-week notice. I scheduled a one-on-one with my Vice President who seemed pretty surprised that I wanted to talk to him. I was brutally honest about everything I had been thinking. When I finished, he leaned back in his chair and broke the entire issue down to me from his point of view. It made total sense.

He basically informed me that I had all of the attributes of a top associate and that I wasn't giving myself a fair chance due to all of my festering frustrations. His insight revealed a lifetime lesson. I was a former top manager in a telemarketing company for four years but had allowed frustration to strip away all of the talent I gained and even taught to others. One of the biggest dangers of that emotion is that it never adds to your ability if it is not used in a motivational direction.

His suggestion was that I move to the department to tour people that did not already own vacation ownership. The department I'd been hired into catered particularly to in-house families which meant they already owned time in a particular resort. Some of the people I talked to owned vacation ownership since the 1980's and their knowledge, my lack of it, and my fearful mindset at the time made it very difficult for me to help them thoroughly.

He said that he would fully support the direction that I chose if I still wanted to resign, but he wanted to transition me to the non-owner division during my last two weeks. His feedback was given in such a calm and genuine manner that I left the meeting with a feeling of peace, assurance and well-being.

I figured that I had nothing to lose by staying a little longer. I went in the next day, in the non-owner division, and got my first sale. More importantly, I was able to give advice to a family which secured their future vacation needs for the rest of their lives. The couple could not afford to go on extravagant family vacations, so financing a lifetime of the freedom to explore world-class accommodations was perfect.

In this new position, I had much more control of the conversation and loved the feeling of accomplishment; however, based on my past performance, I still had the thought in my mind that the move to Maryland would give me the financial security needed for my future. During the next three days, I assisted three more families. Needless to say, in a four day span I did better than what I'd done in my past three months. I had to take a step back and put more thought into this pending move. I felt that everything had turned around for me.

The reality is that with the right attitude I would have accomplished the same success in the previous department with Fairfield. You will always deliver less than what you are capable when you do not start off each endeavor with a clean state. In other words, no matter how dirty your windshield in life may get, it is very important that you clean it before you drive forward. The same advice that I gave the young telemarketers in my previous position became words to live by. *Each minute brings new opportunity.*

Shortly thereafter, I got a call from the same associate who'd introduced me to the Maryland opportunity. The call came on the sixth day after my meeting with my vice-president. I was informed that the Maryland site was shutting down and that I was lucky that I had not officially resigned.

From April 2005 to my retirement in October 2013, my sales performances continued to increase every year in my position at Wyndham. In 2005, with only nine months of actual production because of my slow start, I earned over $185,000 and had no idea that I would be propelled into a tax bracket that required advice from accountants and financial advisors to properly manage. In 2006, implementing some of the lessons learned from my first ride on the train of success, I immediately started investing in the stock market and real estate. Looking back, I used the feelings of uncertainty during the downsizing, as a motivator to ensure that my financial freedom would one day arrive.

I learned several lessons during those five months of my life that I pray can reinforce the principles you already have, or help add to your daily character. By harboring negative emotions you restrict your ability to grow. It was when I realized and released the negative energy I'd allowed to loom and fester inside, regarding my previous employment situation, that I was able to become productive to my new employer. You may feel a certain way about your current employment situation that is not too positive for various reasons. I urge that you find a way to reinvent your mental approach starting now. Is there a way for you to make better use of that opportunity that other people would love to be in called employment? Yes there is. Someone's trash is another person's treasure and the grass always looks greener on the other side. Learn how to make your grass in your field the color that you want it to be.

Only focus on what you can control. My resentment and anger toward an uncontrollable situation prevented me from learning the process and techniques for my position in my new career. If my attitude had been where it should have been, I would have put myself in the right mental state from the beginning. By aggressive daily learning and treating my option at the time like my only option, I would have pushed myself toward greatness earlier.

When you are in a position of leadership you must live by what you teach. The best teachers and coaches actually learn more from their students once they are fully committed to living what they are teaching. After four years of managing sales reps my knowledge should have had me follow the same advice I would always give. I was committed but my mode of thinking reverted when I was in a pessimistic state. Negative thinking was one of the primary reasons I kept coming up with excuses rather than creating solutions. I realized I should have always thought in the most positive manner to progress in life, especially during tough times.

There was not just one instance during this phase where the light bulb came on. It was a series of events during my transition that led to my awakening. Our individual lights should continue to get brighter as we move through life. You may have your own interpretation of the several lessons taught during that phase of my life to help the progression in your world. I started to take a closer look at myself from those life lessons, and currently I treat every new day like my first day of life school. My light bulb really started to shine when I realized that I'd almost walked out on the best opportunity for me at the time because of ignorance. From those days going forward I vowed to separate mentally from my old ways and to never be content with my progress. Life will always throw you unexpected situations; however, you can surely know that there are ways to deal with all adversity to make you a better person afterward.

SUMMARY You have learned that it is very important, that as you make daily life decisions, to stay in a productive mindset to give yourself the best long term advantage, regardless of the circumstance. You are clear that the most unproductive choices are made when you are in a mood that is filled with unhappy emotions, and your best choices are made when you are in a relaxed and clear state of mind. You have learned that you should take full advantage of all of your current opportunities to avoid missing out on future blessings to yourself. You will take some time to sit alone and think about your big picture when unforeseen circumstances take place. You have learned that one of the best ways to control your financial future is to educate yourself on how to properly manage your yearly income.

Chapter 3

What is Your Purpose?

In the life lottery, you can only be
picked if you play to WIN. KD

Twelve unforgettable years have come and gone that have brought me great financial reward. During my journey, I have learned that your purpose should be much more than financially inspired. Wealth is something that everyone deserves, but the true earners in this world had a purpose which had an impact on their path to get their desired financial results. That purpose was to be the best. It is no surprise that the people who are the best in their field are usually the ones that are paid the most. How you start anything controls how you manage through it, so entry into your field needs to be aimed for your overall advantage. If you have only made moves that were directed for monetary compensation or to make ends meet, it's likely you are not putting your heart into your movements. In the book *Outliers,* author Malcolm Gladwell explains how 10,000 hours of aggressive learning in any one field makes you a master. By extension, all employment allows the option for you to gain mastery. For you to fully maximize your daily energy you exhaust, it only makes sense that you gain a full understanding of the entire operation where you work. That applied knowledge allows you to work smarter and not harder, which conserves energy.

Most people do not go into work with the thought of the importance each day has on their big picture. Getting the most productivity out of each day in a twenty year career could be the difference of gaining legacy changing enhancements and $100,000 at a bare minimum. For instance, the president of Wyndham Vacation Ownership used to be a sales representative in Williamsburg, Virginia. His daily focus when he started years ago equaled an income for himself much greater than what he could probably imagine due to his ultimate purpose. You may not have aspirations to run your own company one day but exuding an attitude to get the most out of your place of work separates you from 80% of your work associates. That person who received the promotion over you or performed better simply had a bigger purpose, which is something that you personally control. Even if someone out performs you, knowing that you did your best makes you a better person in the process. Doing your best should be enough but maybe peace of mind in your senior years, or quality of living for your children can put you in the mental place that you need to be in starting now as you read this very sentence.

The danger of clocking in with no intention of growth is that your time, which you cannot get back, is not being used for your long term advancement. When you go into your place of business with a purpose, the habits you practice will always reflect the mindset that you are in training for your next position. The average person never advances in their company or in life because of the lack of that very important principle. Our children, this economy, and ethics in this world are all negatively impacted because of it. This book is geared towards increasing your net worth but as you read you will see that aiming at perfection in all that you do will positively impact your life regardless of where you are or who you are.

To give you an example of how someone can customize their purpose to be in training for their next position, let's take the job description of a server in a restaurant. Have you ever had an experience where it seemed as if your server didn't feel like serving and made your experience feel less than what you expected? If that server's purpose was in line with being the best, you would have had excellent service instead of the substandard service you received. If the server embraced how important each customer's experience was to future business, as if he were the restaurant owner, those unfortunate instances would never occur and the server's tips would considerably increase as well.

When you go into any position with a purpose of striving for perfection, you always earn more, plus other characteristics are enhanced that could be useful to your future as well. A server has the ability to master communication by learning how to adjust to all different kinds of people and get his desired result, a larger tip with repeat business. Certain aspects of psychology can be worked on during that process by taking a customer out of the emotional state that is hindering the desired outcome, and purposefully changing their state to benefit himself and again, the tip. Moving at a fast pace while placing orders quickly can help that server reach a desired target heart rate, which can provide short and long term health benefits. When your purpose is aligned with greatness at all times you win all the way around. It is also no coincidence that those same skills are needed to run a company, live a longer more healthy life, and have better relationships. I hope you are starting to see the UNIVERSAL benefits to your life that can be gained by having a chief purpose. There are a number of extremely successful people in all fields that said they honestly received greater communication skills when they worked in a restaurant for a period of their lives.

Those are just a few examples of how multiple beneficial opportunities lie within a position, and how a position in which many only see limited potential can actually be viewed through a much broader scope. How many other opportunities for growth and development does your current employment allow you to train for that you are not taking advantage of? All habits are created by repetition so the way that you have viewed life is a direct reflection of your past habits. Looking at life through this new lens will definitely help you cover more ground in your growth, but you must start today. As you see serving in a restaurant offers several training opportunities to achieve excellence. In order to benefit from them your purpose for being there has to be aimed in the correct direction. The best part about it is that as you train to make yourself a better person your income potential will also increase.

There are countless opportunities in your daily encounters that you can either recognize as growth opportunities, purposeful growth, self-development, or carelessly overlook them all together by using a non-successful lens. I learned that it is much more strategic to be prepared for the opportunity before it comes, instead of not being prepared and losing out on your chance to take advantage of your big break. Luck is when massive preparation meets opportunity. The principle of purposefully going into each position that you ever have with an open mind to master all of the challenges that come with it will be my recommendation from here on out. I can attest that the principle is proven to work to increase your employee value, gain promotion, earn higher pay, or raise your daily fulfillment. Your purpose may not have started in the correct direction, however starting today you can simply embrace this concept and get much more out of your daily commitments. Please take a moment and write down your current job description and list all the opportunities for future growth that you are going to start mastering today. Don't allow someone in your company, reading this same material who decides to take action, surpass you because you failed to invest the time to map out your future growth.

SUMMARY You are now fully aware that to maximize your daily duties at work it is best to learn as much as you can about the entire operation to prepare yourself for future advancement. You are clear that employment offers preparation for you to one day run your own company by allowing you to constantly gain efficiency at your employment duties. You have learned that it is best to get paid through knowledge that you can take with you to future positions in life instead of just limiting your pay to a check. You have also realized that if you dedicate thousands of hours to a position and not aim at mastery, your success will be limited. This hinders your total advancement in the long run.

Chapter 4

Mindset

Your thoughts are not hidden;
where you are in life clearly shows the world
what has been going on in your head. KD

We all go through ups and downs in life, however, it is how you deal with the twists and turns that determines your outcome in the long run. Having a destructive mindset is never profitable to your growth. Any thought that can lead to any type of harm to yourself or others in the short or long term is destructive. The impact of a destructive mindset is not as immediately severe on your financial circumstances if you work in an hourly or salaried position, because you start earning wages as soon as you clock in whether you show up mentally or not. In the hourly or salaried position it may seem like you are benefiting by the compensation you receive for your time spent, however, without getting character development while in the process you are losing in the long haul. When you are in any type of commission-based employment or entrepreneurship situation, if you don't show up with the correct mental approach you are committing not only emotional but immediate financial suicide.

A positive mindset is important to live successfully regardless of what you do, and it is even more important when it comes to maintaining high performance in any sales industry. What you need to be very clear on is that every day whether you are selling for a living or not you are influencing someone with your ideas. That means that everyone is involved in sales to some degree, directly or indirectly.

The key characteristics that assist with your positive mindset are:

- Self-confidence
- Constant courage in all opportunities
- Willingness to learn at all times
- Habitually being optimistic about any situation
- Completing all tasks that you start

Expecting positive results is one of the most important parts of having a mindset directed toward greatness. Some of the most talented people fail to perform at their maximum level because when it is crunch time, they start doubting themselves which always leads to failure. Doubt is a learned emotion. When you were a baby, before you knew what failure was, you just went for what you wanted without any hesitation. As adults we have the ability to use that same eagerness to our benefit, and failure to tap into that resource will cost you advancement in your future endeavors.

You have complete control of your thoughts and emotions. Two opposing emotions cannot be in your head at the same time with the expectancy of them both being carried out fully. If you are feeling angry and happy at the same time, which is usually not the case, the anger will subtract from you truly being happy and vice versa. The foundation you build your thought process on will be your cure all or your professional death. There are several zombies around you every day that have killed their dreams before they even had a chance to come to fruition because of the thought patterns that they choose to live with. If you are currently not in the mental place that is most beneficial to you, the only way to change it is by constantly inserting new positive thoughts into your head.

The company that you keep on a daily basis plays a crucial part in making a transition from average to exceptional because it is easy to be influenced in the wrong direction by the people you trust the most. Hopefully you are already staying away from the zombies that are not in your direct circle, but sometimes we associate with our close friends and family who are dream killers without a thought. The danger about close dream killers is that they inflict more damage because of your defenses usually being lowered around them, inadvertently allowing the absorption of harmful energy and information. You would be amazed at how many prosperous people fell sharply off the track due to their choice of association. Take an assessment of those who are close to you to determine if they are dream killing zombies. If so, be mindful of, and realign your defenses if necessary. Even if you are in a good place, to eliminate from falling back into bad habits, constant positive mental deposits are necessary. Surrounding yourself with positive people, listening to motivational materials, and quoting positive affirmations are a few ways to ensure your environment is productive.

You can be content with what you have but you should never be content with who you are as a person. This is a crucial component in how greatly you succeed. The reason so many people who achieve greatness don't maintain it is because of contentment. Your will to win has to be greater than the win itself. Success can remain continuous if you remain humble and continue to learn more about yourself and life itself on a daily basis. If you don't know where to continue the self-improvement journey after reading this, look back on your life experiences. Once you analyze your past, the present becomes apparent. Go to the library and search out materials that will help you learn from others who have survived similar experiences and discover from their path how to positively turn yours around or how to push yourself into a new league of personal and professional performance. I came up with a rule for success in 2008 called A WINNER'S TEN MINUTES. Celebrate your accomplishment for two and figure out how to get better in the next eight. It started for my quarterly recognition but eventually I carried that mindset into all victories on a daily basis. That is how I have continuously increased performance in all areas of my life and sales ever since.

Fear is also one of the biggest obstacles that must be overcome to truly excel in life. Unless you were put in a situation where something happened to you because of an accident or circumstances beyond your control, most fears are based upon a false perception of reality. Even in cases where fear did form because of a real event, fear can be overcome by constant mental rehabilitation. The most common fears that come with the sales industry and life are the fear of failure, fear of people, fear of change, and the fear of the unknown future. All fears are conquerable and the simplest way that I recommend to overcome any growth limitations instilled by fear is by educating yourself on the background of what has caused that fear. For every fear that one may have, there are others who've met that same fear with courage and overcame it, so it is possible for you to overcome it as well. You have to be real with yourself because only you know what you truly fear. The absolute worst thing that you can do is recognize the fear, do nothing about it and let your response to that fear become habitual.

A major part of your results in life is based upon how well you communicate with people, and if you limit who you are comfortably able to speak to, your success will be limited. I knew a young lady once who truly had a fear of communicating with certain races of people due to her background. After self-education, she realized that her fear was only due to ignorance and from what her father taught her. If the views of our parents go against successful thinking models, we cannot carry those restrictive thoughts forward. She told me that what she learned after confronting the source of her fear was that whenever you fear something you are placing chokeholds on possible blessings. Ironically her husband ended up being a person from one of the races that she once feared. Her biggest advancement in her view of life was that she realized all people are equal regardless of their ethnic background. They now have two beautiful children and they provide marriage counseling in their neighborhood church. You can learn something from all existence so the fear of anything simply limits your growth, which internally locks you down.

How you look at life as a whole started when you were younger. Your view of how to have a successful mindset is usually based upon what you were exposed to through your first thirteen years of life. It was during those years that your main belief system was constructed and those core values helped lead you to where you currently are at this moment. There are several questions that you must ask yourself and be honest when you answer because the future direction of your life depends on it.

- Are you following your parent's footsteps down the wrong direction in your life?
- Were your parents the type that complained about how much they worked and how they were under paid?

- Was underachievement a part of what you were exposed to regularly?
- Did your parents struggle to pay bills? On the other hand did you get everything you asked for as a child and never really wanted for anything?
- Was your entire life planned out for you from pre-school to college without any input from you?
- Was your vision of success established by someone else and did not include your own self-established goals?
- Were you unintentionally institutionalized to think that doing the least to just get by was the best way to beat the system?
- Were all the employed people in your surrounding in an hourly or salary position?
- Was quitting and moving to another scenario considered the best fix for troubled times?

I admit that my answer was yes to a few of those questions when I did my self-evaluation. Through being honest and deprograming my mental dashboard, I started to see lights in my tunnel. All may not apply to you but as you can see, these are questions that need to be answered regardless of your family's financial status. The number of people that do not even have a clue why they cannot progress from their current life status is staggering. Simply trimming the edges will not fix a plant that is growing in the wrong direction; the problem must be addressed at the root. The dangers of not educating yourself beyond the realities that you were dealt are that your full potential is at risk of not being met because of your lack of exposure. I have a friend who literally received everything that he wanted his entire life from his parents, and when they died he had no idea of how to be self-reliant. It truly was a blessing that he didn't need for anything while they were living; however, without learning how to be self-sufficient he actually became extremely dependent on their help without realizing it until they were gone. The fact is that you do not have to follow the footsteps of what you were exposed to if the path is not heading in the correct successful direction. Overall success is not defined by a monetary value, but as your awareness increases you should make better strategic moves to ensure your net worth increases as well. Being emotionally, spiritually, physically and mentally balanced are all equal parts of true success and realizing from where your values stem are very important contributors to achieving it. You must build upon all of the positives and all of the negatives must be totally eliminated.

If you have ever heard the saying "knowing is half of the battle", then this is the chapter that puts some true meaning behind it. If you are looking through eyes that are blinded by anger, confusion, doubt, complacency and negative energy, yet don't realize that your life only brings what you visualize, the time is now to get back on the right track. The best part about realizing the truth is that it can be fixed with rehabilitation. Looking in the mirror is the first step to self-development and then creating a burning desire to self-educate is the next step. It may seem scary to take a closer look and face your hidden demons but the results to your life in the long run will be much more frightening if you look away. Once you gain the knowledge, then simply applying the methods that have already been proven to change the undesired thought process handles the rest.

Let me put this in perspective; I am not taking a factory made Honda Civic, which is a very dependable car, and racing in the Daytona 500. The reason is that in order to win a race of that caliber, the car I use has to be built for extremely high speed performance. That is exactly the same rule that applies to your mental approach for your performance in life. When you are in an industry that rewards people who have certain characteristics, it only makes sense to build the proper mental strength to super perform in those traits. No matter what you do for a living, molding a base of characteristics that reflect positivity at all times should be mandatory for you.

Your mindset is the engine that runs your mental car. If the engine is clogged up with corrosive and toxic materials that are damaging to its overall performance, you must get it diagnosed and repaired in order for it to run efficiently. If you do not it may run for a while but it will not run at the performance level needed, and eventually it will shut down. You are the only certified mechanic that can truly work on your mental car, and where you end up on a daily basis is totally dependent on the quality of your craftsmanship and quality of your work. If you have realized in this chapter that your car is about to break down, running on fumes or not running fast enough, take the personal initiative and do an engine flush.

If not for yourself, do it for the people looking up to you. The last thing that you want to do is set your future children, children, family members or friends up for failure because of the pace you've set. If you are around people in your life who are not clear in their life direction, they must want to get on track to be associated with you. You do not have ignorance to blame because I just painted the picture for you to see your light. If you are willing to grow, I congratulate you because the first step on your path to freedom has just been mapped out.

This chapter of the book is so critical and without true self-analysis your life has invisible limits that are placed on it. A lion born in the zoo only knows life in captivity because all he has been exposed to is the cage where he exists. If the lion is never exposed to the freedom of the jungle he will simply exist without knowing what else is out there. That rule applies to us human beings and my goal is to motivate you to simply look outside your cage by realizing where and why it was created in the first place. The only limits that humans have are the ones that are acknowledged.

SUMMARY You have learned that your mind is the sole controller of how you succeed in every action that you ever participate in. You are very clear that in order for you to achieve success, you have to remain positive at all times, and implement certain characteristics into your daily habits no matter the circumstance. You are aware that fear in any form is conquerable and to eliminate it you must completely understand its source. You have learned that you must grow on the positive traits that were given to you during your childhood, and also continuously self-develop to eliminate all limiting behaviors that you were exposed to. You are aware that your view of life is based upon your past and you will constantly increase your awareness by never becoming complacent in your way of thinking.

Chapter 5

The Science of Selling

We as a people are much more similar than we are different. The first step in adjusting to the masses is getting to truly know who you are. KD

Before we get further into this life change, I need to make sure that you truly understand my science on the process of selling. The best part about this section is that it combines my experience of how people buy ideas, services and products regardless of cost. Every time you persuade anyone to do anything, it is because they were sold on your idea. Once you learn how to move anyone in the direction that you want them to go, you will attain constant success regardless of your profession. The quicker you realize how important the art of communication is to your life progression, the faster you will advance. We have become so accustomed to just walking into an establishment and buying what we want. The ease of buying items is one of the biggest issues when it comes to someone truly understanding how to succeed at becoming a professional communicator, and persuading someone to buy their idea. The action of buying the idea and the action of selling the idea are connected but you must understand how they differ.

When you go into the mall just mainly looking around and something catches your eye, you walk into the store and buy the item. The cashier that takes your form of payment did sell the item to you, but you already had a plan to buy it because of emotions in your head that made you want the item. You might have needed the item, thought it looked good, and saw that it was on sale, but by the time you went to the cashier the decision to purchase was already made. The possible emotions that moved you were fear of missing out on a sale, the pride of how you would look in the item, or necessity which could also be looked at as a fear of the item no longer being available at a later time. Knowing how to draw those different feelings out of someone are the initial steps of learning persuasion. Remember, in most careers involving sales the customer did not intend to make a purchase, which means you cannot expect for them to come in and hand you money as though you are a cashier. You have to figure out the emotions that need to be involved for the prospect to make that decision.

In order to know the emotions involved to help persuade, extensive research has to be done in the industry you are involved in. If I am the owner of "KINJA'S ATTORNEY AT LAW" and I specialize in divorces, it is my responsibility to know all of the emotions associated with couples who divorce, the emotions of the entire family and how to deal with all people who go through it. There are many great firms that do not get to showcase their talent because that first consultation does not emotionally lead the husband or wife to want that firm to represent their case. I hope you are starting to understand how mastering the UNIVERSAL TALK LAWS will increase results no matter the situation or circumstance.

The person that you are attempting to persuade has to be in a total state of comfort, because if a person is in a defensive state you will always get resistance. Ideas, products, and services will never be truly considered if the person feels threatened in any way. To ensure that you are being received you must make sure that the prospect is at ease. That is also a process that includes knowing how to draw out certain emotions, which is the universal root of learning how to persuade. As you will see in all of my following examples, the person that was moved into a certain direction had to be comfortable before the emotion that swayed them became engaged.

There is only one more investment property in an area where you will be able to instantly triple your money. The agent discloses that there are two more investors scheduled to look at the property in three days, and after looking at it, you hastily make an offer to take it off the market as soon as possible. One of the emotions attached to that entire situation sold you on moving quickly to avoid losing out.

A four year old comes up to her mother whining "Ma, can I please get some more?" The mother wants to say no but says yes anyway. The mother was sold on giving her child more of whatever the child asked for. No money was exchanged, but an idea was sold from a persistent little child. What emotions made that mother give in to the child?

Every one that votes is usually sold the ideas of that party or candidate they are voting for to help their personal situation. What are the emotions that sell the millions of voters to put someone in office?

The person that finally gives in to going out on the date with the person who keeps asking them at the gym was sold on the idea of planning a lunch outing. What was the feeling that finally after three requests sold that person on taking them up on their offer?

You put a $2 tip in the jar of the person playing an instrument very well at the festival; you were sold that they earned your money because of their talent. You could have just kept walking but you stopped, dug in your pocket and gave your hard earned money. Why?

In your own understanding reflect on the above examples and you will rapidly realize how to increase your sales ability. Take a few minutes and answer each of my questions in the previous examples. If you understand how and why those emotions were presented, you are getting a higher yet simplistic learning of the sales process. In each example there were feelings of comfort that allowed the follow-up emotions to take place. For instance, in the example with the mother, prior to giving in to what the child wanted, she had to have a feeling of concern for the child's needs to even make that consideration.

There are endless opportunities that you can learn from daily to help increase your emotional awareness in yourself and others. Once you can figure out how to trigger different emotions in your particular situation, there are no more limits on your capability to persuade anyone.

A master communicator studies and understands all of the different emotions that cause the prospects they are talking to go in the direction that is needed. There are six primary root emotions that are used when someone decides to purchase something which are as follows:

1) **Fear**. If I don't buy this now I will not have a chance in the future.
2) **Greed**. I don't need more but if I buy more now I will be rewarded in the end.
3) **Envy**. If they can buy it so can I.
4) **Shame**. If I don't buy this I am going to look unintelligent.
5) **Pride**. Once I buy this I am going to look better than everyone else.
6) **Altruism**. If I buy this it is going to help someone out.

There are several times when two or more of these emotions are engaged at the same time for a single purchase. For instance, in the example using the investment property, fear, greed, and pride were all included in that purchase decision. Knowing that other investors were coming instilled fear that one of the other investors would get it first, the greed of not needing another investment property yet knowing it will greatly pay off in the end, and the pride of making a wise financial investment were all involved. The unsuccessful communicator believes that they can just simply make someone want to purchase by explaining benefits, and that is not by any means a way to stay consistent in communicating with people. Understanding the emotional drivers behind purchase decisions will be one of the most critical pieces of your progression and as you develop the skills, your emotional intelligence must increase as well along the way.

In order to manage anyone's emotions
you must begin by mastering your own. KD

SUMMARY You are very clear that the better you communicate, the more you will succeed in life. You know that it is to your advantage to understand the true science of selling whether you sell for a living or not. You are also aware that learning how to persuade anyone requires them to be in a total state of ease, to give you the proper ability to figure out their chief buying motive. You understand that the art of salesmanship has more to do with learning how all people think versus solely an exchange of currency. The six root emotions that cause people to make buying decisions are now understood and you will use this knowledge to you and your customer's advantage. As you go through life you will constantly increase your understanding of how you think to better grasp how others feel.

Chapter 6

The Mindset of the Customer

*In order to fill up the bucket, you have to first patch
up the holes that are in the bottom of it. KD*

As I further prepare you for a consistently successful life of communication, I hope that you have realized that the first step is to master thyself. The ability to master yourself is a never ending journey that continuously helps you to understand all that you come in contact with. Once you begin this process you reap emotional wealth, which is the most important wealth you can possess.

Misunderstanding the customer is one of the reasons why the turnover rate is so high in commission-based sales. To avoid contributing to the attrition rates you must understand why there are so many losses in the first place. In school, you know what to expect to a certain degree, and in that hourly based or salaried position, you are given a description of your duties which allow you to somewhat prepare for what you have to do to receive financial compensation. In commission only sales, you mix not knowing what to expect due to the vast array of customer types, with the uncertainty of the pay that you will receive, and unless you approach this way of life with a proven strategy, you will not last. In order to consistently remain successful you must begin the path of mastering your own emotions which will allow you to lead that customer down the path that is best for the both of you. The better you realize how the person or people on the other side of the table think, the further down the road of success you will go.

To help you understand the customer's mindset, let's explore the thoughts they have about how you are going to be when they meet you, and the fears they have that cause them to walk away from taking advantage of your idea, product or service:

- I bet we get a Mr. Know-It-All
- I hope they do not have us in here all day
- I have a lot of questions and I hope they get answered
- The last time we came I had a horrible/positive experience; I wonder how today is going to turn out
- I have all of the facts; they better not try to mislead me

Here are a few reasons potential customers or clients walk away in the end without taking advantage of the idea, service or product:

- I can always come back if I really want to.
- I have too many other priorities to handle and this is not one of them.
- I am getting older so I need to start spending much more conservatively.
- It is not going to work as easily as he says it will.
- She had too many holes in her story. I did not believe one word she said.

- He didn't seem to know anything. He had to keep bringing someone over to answer questions that I believe he should have known.

In the upcoming chapters I will share some techniques that when properly implemented and combined with other key learnings will eliminate these fears during your interaction. The purpose of this chapter is for you to gain a clearer understanding of what the customer sees and perceives that would hinder a successful close, and what your preparation should be to overcome it. Understand that they are perceptions that the customer should actually have, and many times predicated upon numerous communication interactions where the presenter wasn't keen enough to consider and address the customer's comfort level, or lack thereof. It may not have been intentional for the presenter to discomfort the customer, but because the customer's mindset was not factored into the presentation, the delivery, regardless of the intent, left an unpleasant taste in the customer's mouth.

To effectively master the art of communication with a prospect, it is very important that you realize their mindset when you interact with them. How they are thinking in the beginning and in the end are equally important. The definition of a prospect can apply to either a business or personal contact, so do not limit these practices to your place of business. My point is that when you are interacting with your friends, family, spouse and/or business associates, the same courtesy given to a prospect should apply to benefit those relationships as well. All people want to feel important and listened to. When you master delivering total comfort to all people that you communicate with, life becomes so much more rewarding and your net worth will increase.

The harsh reality is that most people are not emotionally

intelligent. In order for you to maneuver through getting your points across, it is critical that you become more fluent daily in speaking to all emotions that come your way. Some emotional languages are more complex to interpret than others and to begin translation you must know what emotional languages you generally speak.

An emotional language is the way a person uses their emotions in a given situation. Are you the type of person who only interacts comfortably with a certain type of personality? If you compare a successful salesperson to a person who speaks several foreign languages, you will see they both have more freedom to properly communicate because they can adapt to more people. Researching the hundreds of cultures in this world will give you great insight to add to your understanding of human nature.

The key to succeeding in communicating with another person or other people is being able to pick up signals that clue you in on what they did that morning and the night before. Unless you have special powers that we are not going to talk about in this book, that may be a slight challenge at this point; however, factoring that thought into your mind as you approach your client will be tremendously helpful as you prepare to speak their language. There are several life challenges that people deal with on a daily basis and if it is apparent that something is wrong in the beginning, it could lead to a very good introductory conversation if your mind is in the right place. For instance, addressing a look of anger or distress on someone's face always led me to ask a few questions like "I may be wrong but you seem to be the type of person that is usually smiling, so this is probably out of character for you. Is there anything I can do to make your day go a little better? What happened; and if it has anything to do with how my staff treated you today please give me a name." The worst thing that could happen is that you switch someone's mental state, which in turn adds versatility to your persuasion abilities. The unsuccessful thinkers come up with reasons for why their prospects won't be interested before they even start, while the strategists figure out how to make it work to their advantage. It also shows that you are a person who is considerate enough to even notice, and some genuine ice breaking will stem from it, as well. By simply being aware of their possible disposition is not enough. You must cater your interaction to addressing it in a way that promotes ease and great conversation will follow.

There are several different personalities you will run into so to help simplify the process it is best that principles are used to guide your every move. So far we have learned that you must not be afraid to address any underlining turmoil and adjust to their emotional language. You also have to be prepared for the unexpected because throughout my twelve years of successful communication I rarely got exactly what I expected, only surprises and more surprises. People are all unique and the master sales person embraces the following realities instead of running away from them:

- The average prospect uses no guidelines to help them interact
- Most people are not emotionally intelligent
- You have to learn how to adjust to all personalities

Regardless of whether you are stunted by your own growth or the lack of growth in others (customers or your associates), bondage, figuratively or literally, is not acceptable in any situation. Adapting to others, mental preparedness and maintaining optimism verses pessimism are key fundamentals to consistent success.

It may be hard to believe at some points in our lives, but all people have some greatness in them. Being able to program yourself to find it in all people is what makes you great in the process. The problem is that as people suffer and endure trying times, they incur wounds in the process, which usually do not heal correctly. Due to their lack of proper healing, their defenses start to build, and that is what causes the reactions that you deal with on a day-to-day basis when interacting with other people. If you have realistic expectations of becoming a master communicator, it is imperative that you realize these facts. There have been hundreds of instances where the troubled customer I met turned out to be one of the best people I have ever run into. I just had to take time to understand how the path they travelled led them to me.

You would be amazed at what you could deal with if you fully understood what made you tick and the reasons why. The better you know thyself and what you are made of, the stronger you become mentally. That strength causes you to become a wiser individual and the range of situations that you can adapt to will become much larger. It sounds simple and it truly is, however, due to complacency the average person doesn't take the time to widen their range.

Never fight fire with fire. I have turned more angry customers around, who were only angry due to previous experiences by smiling and calmly asking questions, rather than frowning and raising my voice as a form of retaliation. Once you insert the "how can I serve you?" attitude into your exchanges, the results that you receive are stress relieving because you now begin taking control by giving what you demand in return. You have less of a right to be obnoxious to a person who is just so genuinely nice to you. Another benefit of this principle is that no one can take control of your emotions and you become less susceptible to someone throwing you off of your game. It is a very simple approach to life; however, at least one of the parties involved has to exhibit emotional intelligence for it to work. Just remember the saying... Sticks and stones can break my bones but words can never hurt me... unless you allow them to.

As the professional who is welcoming a client/prospect into your establishment, it is your responsibility to take any negativity and make it positive. Regardless of the circumstance, you have to make the customer happy and that is the bottom line. The companies/people that understand that flourish while the ones that don't, fail. If the root of your business is not built on that foundation you may do great temporarily but that superior performance cannot be sustained.

I thrive on simple ways to conquer challenges, so I am going to give you a secret that I finally figured out in relation to customers. First, I will detail the types of buyers you usually run into:

- The shopper who claims they are just browsing
- The analytical buyer who wants to mathematically examine the purchase
- The get-down-to-business buyer who constantly rushes you to get to the bottom line
- The perfect buyer who comes in with an open mind, ready to purchase after you have presented the service/product well.

The perfect buyer scenario is very rare and expecting to encounter that type of buyer is a big mistake when entering into sales. You must prepare for the most difficult situations, which believe it or not, starts turning even the most complex customers into the simplest customers to communicate with.

What type of buyer are you? The selling style that you present is usually reflective of the type of buyer you are, which can be a barrier if you are talking to a buyer of a different type. Sometimes you have more than one type of buyer in the same person, or a husband and wife combination who are different types of buyers within their marriage. The secret is getting to know the person behind the buyer type by asking strategic questions and listening intently to all that is said.

SUMMARY You have learned that every person you have contact with is a customer and that having a total understanding of how that person feels helps you to communicate clearly. You are clear that giving each customer a feeling of importance while you listen helps to best attain your end goal. You are aware that your success in communication will broaden as you comfortably learn to adapt to emotional languages. You have learned that it is much more effective to be totally respectful and courteous at all times regardless of how the customer interacts, and to remain in total control. You are aware of the different types of buyers and that getting to the root of what type of person they are is the best way to navigate down the road of persuading at all times. You are now aware that as you master your emotions, you master how to deal with all circumstances.

Chapter 7

How to Start Your Day as a UNIVERSAL Talker

The best way to wake up is with a target in mind. Compete with the person you were yesterday and in the process you will win daily. Success is habitual. KD

The first and most important yet often overlooked step to the beginning of a successful day is a pre-set plan for the day, proper night's rest, and a well-balanced breakfast the following morning. The strategic planning of your day is so critical because your actions the night before will align with your next day's outcome; being well rested always adds to your energy throughout any day; and it is a statistical fact that those who eat breakfast in the morning perform better than those who don't.

For instance, there is a fool-proof plan in regards to getting out of a slump that fits perfect in this section. If I did not execute on a sale due to a communication failure on my part, I had a sequence of events that I'd follow that evening to ensure I would not make the mistake again, and go into my next day expecting better results. I would document the benefits that I attempted to convey, explore the reasons they chose not to go forward, brainstorm about other ways to have completed the transaction and then most importantly do something productive to get all of my frustration out. The gym was usually my way to not only maintain my health, but also release any exasperation and ensure that I did not carry any of the turmoil from the previous day into the next. Create a brief list of positive actions that you will follow to implement your own fool-proof plan on your rough days.

- _____

- _____

- _____

- _____

- _____

I guarantee that those types of days will decrease and you will turn turmoil into triumph. All slumps take place when no effective plan is constructed and you carry old turmoil into a new day which is counterproductive.

Who you associate with on a daily and nightly basis is also extremely important because remember, your mindset needs to be in the correct place to excel on a consistent basis. Jim Rohn, a motivational speaker and self-help guru, says that you are a mixture of the 5 people that are closest to you. The harsh reality in many cases is that you might need to re-evaluate who you have in your world if you are aiming for improving your quality of life and they are not. Before eliminating their presence at least attempt to bring them on board. If they resist you must move on to protect your future. I am a true believer that the company you keep is only as strong as the weakest link.

Now that we have gotten the basics out of the way, it is time to really explore the traits associated with starting your day with super success in mind. The mindset in which you start your day has to embrace the blessing of being able to freely leave your home and go to your place of employment/entrepreneurship where you chose to work. Just that simple step is often overlooked, but approaching your day understanding that there are people in this world who would give a great deal to be in your shoes will cause you to feel both humbled and urgent at the same time. If you are waking up dreading the thought of delivering the service that you signed up to do, there is some self-reflection that must take place. You need to find a higher purpose for getting up each day, or change your life direction immediately.

Once you get into your vehicle, walk, ride your motorcycle/bicycle or fly to your place of employment, you enter into a very important time which, if used correctly, can positively impact your results. I used to get into character in my vehicle by role playing with myself. Practice makes perfect and what turns you into a master is time spent increasing your skill level. That ability to acquire mastery should not be left to just when you are in your place of employment. I may have looked funny to others who glanced at me while I was en route to work, but the results of my role-play were positive. Whoever

I came in contact with during the day was able to benefit from my practice. The number of people on this earth who just show up to their daily employment opportunity, with no mental preparation needs to decrease. Once you start the habit of getting into character before all projects you'll encounter, you will be propelled into places you have never imagined.

For example, if you are a salesperson you need to be enthusiastic, upbeat, emotionally intelligent, very vocal and persistent and if on a particular day you feel tired, annoyed, and really non-verbal it only makes sense that you force yourself into the character that properly suits the role that will deliver the best results. After twenty-one days of getting into character you will create habits that will make all that you do on a daily basis more effective. To take a step further, you may need to ask yourself some personal questions about what you have going on in your life to make you feel negative or unhappy and then answer them. If your household is causing you to leave your home in an unproductive state of mind, then look at whatever you have going on and fix it immediately. As Einstein said, doing the same thing over and over again and expecting different results is the definition of insanity.

Another great way to start (and end) your day is to read inspirational literature or listen to self-help audiobooks, and make it a daily habit. I used to only read in the evenings because my days were always so busy and unpredictable, which of course is better than not reading at all, however, it was no mere coincidence that since 2009 when I maximized my opportunity to absorb more material during my daily commute to and from work by listening to audiobooks that my performance in life and at the office exploded in the way that it did. During my drive, which was typically between one to two hours a day, there were no outside factors or unpredictable happenings to circumvent my plan to gain knowledge. Over the course of a few years, I was able to subject myself to more than 1400 hours of personal and financial development by utilizing an opportunity most people overlook every day. My life will never be the same because of it.

Understanding the meaning of the term congruency will also assist in this process. This refers to your subconscious thoughts being aligned with what you say. The only person you fool is yourself if your words do not reflect how you feel. Once you can tap into your true purpose and align your outside wants with your inside thoughts anything that you ask for will be given to you. If your purpose for doing your daily duties causes your motivation to happen from within you will have a base to build upon. You have to believe in what you are getting up to do, and if you do not believe it, remember this truth: *If all else fails fake it 'til you make it.* There are treasures and opportunities within your reach daily so train yourself by first looking at your cup of life as halfway full instead of halfway empty.

The best part about my philosophy on starting your day in a positive frame of mind is that it will boost your productivity in sales but most importantly in life. You will feel better and everyone that you pass the positivity to will feel better, as well. Your day usually goes by much faster which is much better than the alternative. Spread this information to all the people you come in contact with. You are only as blessed as the amount of others you bless.

Your first thoughts when you wake up determine how well your daily life food is digested. You will only be hungry if you ate right the day before. KD

SUMMARY You are very clear that the start of your day is essential to how productive you are throughout. You have learned that the people who you are around daily, directly impact how you think and to help elevate yourself you will be selective about those that you associate with on a daily basis. You have learned that to maximize your day it is best to reflect on the millions who would love to trade places with you. You have learned to mentally prepare yourself with constant positive thought insertions to yourself during your commute to your place of employment. You are very clear that your mental habits, if unproductive, can be realigned by instilling new habits that will replace the old ones in time.

Chapter 8

Greeting

*The first few minutes of any interaction
can put the weight of the world on a person's
shoulders or take it off. KD*

Throughout the next five chapters, I am now going to detail individually, starting with the greeting, the five universal steps to get a person or a group of people to move in the direction that you would like. The way you deliver the steps may need slight adjustment, depending on the type of product/service/idea that is being presented.

Message to yourself before you greet your customer: *The people that I am about to meet are good people and the message that I will convey will be delivered exactly the way I intend it to be. My ending goal will be attained no matter what gets thrown in my path. I am an unstoppable force and can adjust to anyone regardless of their background. I am a chameleon.*

To give yourself a true chance at a proper customer greeting you must understand that pre-judging is absolutely one of the biggest mistakes that are made when it comes to delivering sales or customer service. Regardless of the reason, if you do not totally eliminate that trait it will negatively impact your results.

I have a short story that will show you how it will work against you. A server saw a couple enter a restaurant where he worked. Because of how they looked he hoped that they did not sit in his section. Of course, they did sit in his section and he delivered far from the best service. First of all, his purpose to serve was overcome by his prejudice towards the customers. Secondly, because of his state of mind, his attitude definitely showed in his treatment towards the couple. The tip they left reflected the service that he gave to them. A similar looking couple walked in and they too sat in his section. His head could have popped from the anger, and once again his service and his tip were equivalent. What are the lessons to be gained from this mistake that takes place daily?

What did this server expect customers to look like when he decided to work in a public restaurant? Where did he get the thought in his head that he could actually modify the quality of service he provided based upon how customers look? All people should be treated the way you desire to be treated, at all times. If that server didn't pre-judge in the first place there is a great possibility that both of his tips would have been better. Your internal emotions transfer regardless of whether they are positive or negative. You have to train yourself to maximize your abilities to make the most out of every possibility. You may not realize it but when you have negative thoughts about any person, you act slightly different toward him or her. Sometimes you may not even notice it but the other person usually does. Remember that the way you view people did not form overnight, so if you are a victim of ignorance that has been passed down to you, begin widening your view of life today. It can literally cost you millions in revenue if you do not.

Another basic foundation that I have built my success on when it comes to the beginning contact with a customer, whether in person or by phone, is as follows: *You must close them with your opening.* This simply means that the first impression you deliver has to fit exactly with the comfort that you are aiming to give at the close. Depending on the service you are providing there are several ways that the opening can take place. One of the essential elements in any introduction is your appearance, regardless of whether you are talking to someone in person or not. It is proven that your confidence is increased when you are dressed for success. So many telemarketing agents miss out on developing mental strength, believing that they can lower their standard of appearance because they are not seen by the prospect. I recommend that you follow this rule regardless of how your message is delivered. Right before you begin your interaction look in a mirror, say your pre-greeting message, and then it is show time.

When initial contact is made firm eye contact is a must for a couple of key reasons. It shows respect on your part and it also allows you to start the analysis of who you are dealing with immediately. Ask the prospect how they would like you to address them and you will be amazed at the difference in comfort throughout the entire interaction by simply addressing the client in the fashion that they desire. A smile is mandatory and usually attracts one directed back to you or tells you very early that they are not in a happy state which should be addressed right then in a comfortable way. A simple question to ask if you sense that your bright smile has been met with anger is: "I apologize; I usually get a warm welcome when I meet people so I must have given off energy that I didn't intend to. Did I do something to offend you without my knowledge?" That question will give you what you need to know almost every time about why they are frowning without you being confrontational in any way.

Genuinely showing concern about how far they traveled to get to you or where they live, an item of clothing or jewelry that they are wearing that you are interested in, or simply asking how long they have been waiting instantly starts off the process with the correct tone. An introduction of yourself and explaining why you are the one talking to them also customizes the experience. The introduction should not be a chance to brag on yourself but more of a quick snap shot of your journey to get to them. Every family that I ever spoke to throughout my career knew about my dear love for my mother and how the Air Force brought me to Virginia in my introduction. Depending on the service you provide, the length and detail of your introduction may differ. The more the customer looks at you as a real person, the lower their defense will be which increases your chances of getting through to them. Another very important tip that instantly lowers the defense in anyone early in a meeting is to ask a genuine question that allows them to teach you something about an area that they have expertise in. Because you just met, that will usually be a follow-up question after finding out something about the client that allows you to ask it in the first place. For instance, if you're talking to a couple and they both have "25 Years of Marriage" T-shirts on, asking them how to have a successful marriage would allow them to give you some advice. You actually are following a proven success principle when you do this by gaining new insight from another person's eyes which can only help you become a wiser individual in the long run.

Laughter is also a great way to ease any natural tension in a greeting process. As you read earlier, I lost 100 pounds during my journey to freedom and I used to show my guests my before picture in the introduction stage. It was a great way to draw out some smiles of amazement, and in some cases due to the customer attempting to lose weight as well, it gave me a chance to answer their questions in regards to how I did it. Light humor about my past has worked well for me, however you must be extremely comfortable with the topic you choose to laugh about. Please keep the customer's comfort in mind and stay away from any topic that could be considered offensive to anyone.

Enthusiasm is a must throughout and it spreads to the customer once you adjust it correctly to the type of person you meet. I have seen people fresh out of training who had no idea about the details of their product, lead customers to a completed sale because of raw enthusiasm. The tone of voice you use, coupled with your belief in what you are saying, transfers a feeling of security to the customer that always increases their comfort level.

There are two forms of enthusiasm: passive and active. In the beginning, your enthusiasm is usually passive and becomes active as you get into your later steps. I am usually an active enthusiast overall and that includes strong forms of passion in my delivery mixed with high energy, however, due to the various types of clients, I make adjustments accordingly. Passive enthusiasts are usually much calmer. Knowing which type you are naturally allows you to fill in the necessary voids to complete your versatility. The overall perception the customer gets regardless, is that you are focused on your business and you are there specifically for one purpose, which is to serve their needs.

Genuine statements of appreciation for customers or clients in your establishment and an expression of how important they are as a consumer are also very key elements that have to be present from your welcome to the end of your presentation. When you look at the entire sales process and understand the emotions that are usually running through the prospect's head it makes sense to diffuse all defenses as early as possible. You do this by making their experience with you the most comfortable interaction they have ever been involved in. The best part about these practices I have found is that you are actually training for how all of your life interactions should be in the first place. If in your tunnel of view you find it difficult to do, it is time that you look in the mirror and start asking yourself some questions about how you perceive life. Regardless of how negative your past experiences have been, only you can take the proper self-developing steps to create a better view for yourself. You are baking a sales cake and in order for your cake to cook properly, each ingredient has to be measured precisely. The greeting ingredient is very critical to the outcome. If it is not mixed in correctly the cake will not taste pleasant in the end.

If you exude the right amount of confidence in your delivery, mixed with making the person comfortable beyond their normal experience, you will have made a genuine bond. The second time I bought an investment property it was from an agent in Newport News, Virginia, Keith Canty and I realized that it was possible to want to do business with someone due to the comfort delivered in the greeting. He built such a rapport when we first met that I made up my mind that I would do business with him before we even looked at the first house. That is the type of feeling that you should attempt to deliver in all greetings from this point on.

As you prepare to move to the next step, keep in mind that what you say to someone and what is understood by that person is usually very different. The way to avoid getting all the way to the end of your presentation and the person saying that they don't quite understand is to do regular temperature checks. What has worked great for me is to ask the customer if they understood what was just said, and sometimes I have even asked for them to repeat what I just said in their own words. It also helps to offer a notepad because as they write, your message is being both heard and visualized, which increases their level of understanding.

Quick tip: If you treat all customers the way you'd like to be treated you'll always deliver better results. I am going to end the greeting section with two questions that I want you to answer honestly. Only you can answer the questions and regardless of the answer it will make a life lasting point to you and your family. If you worked at a car lot, selling cars and Oprah Winfrey or Bill Gates came in looking for a vehicle, would you treat them any differently than the way you would treat someone else, because of their financial picture? If you met either one of them would it be right for them to speak down to you because you have not yet made a billion dollars? Regardless of your answers, the cold hard facts are that there are several people with millions or billions of dollars that appear to be in humble circumstances and are not famous. On the other hand, some of the best people that I have ever met are working class individuals that have also contributed to this world in major ways. How much money you have (or don't have) should not dictate how you are treated or how you treat anyone else. Everyone should be treated like royalty regardless of their financial background. To avoid ever being in a position where you make a costly wrong guess about someone's position, greet everyone with total respect. You will be taking another vital step toward becoming a master UNIVERSAL communicator.

SUMMARY You have learned that all people should be treated the way you would like to be without any forms of pre-judging at any time, especially during the initial contact. You have learned the essential first steps in the greeting process regardless of what service/product/idea you are promoting. You have learned to use your smile as a great way to express your gratitude for the initial contact and also as a way to detect if there are any lingering issues. You have learned that being enthusiastic spreads to the customer and regardless of whether it is passive or active it must be present.

Chapter 9

The Discovery

Depending on your vision and listening skills,
the jungle can bring one of the best experiences
you have ever had in life or the very last. KD

The entire purpose of the discovery is to realize early on what solutions you will be able to provide to the customer. Whether they have interest or not, creativity is very important in this step, especially if the customer did not come in inquiring about adding a product/service/idea into their life. If the greeting was implemented and delivered correctly your chances of the prospect being completely honest with you during your discovery are much higher. It is essential that you have great knowledge of all of the available benefits and potential issues the average customer in your industry could be presented with, which will help with your discovery questions. It is also crucial in this stage to find out what their personal direction is so that you can eliminate any objections before you recommend a solution.

For instance, if a prospect is indecisively walking around a car lot, it is imperative that the correct questions are asked during the discovery. The average car dealer is going to ask about price range in their discovery because in their head, they do not want to waste time. Instead, the primary purpose for the vehicle, how many miles they plan to drive a day, the prospect's best and worst vehicle driving experiences, and their driving record would just be a start if I were facilitating a discovery. Knowing the best and worst vehicle driving experiences, average mileage and purpose would help me better customize available options. I would also inform them that the only purpose of the driving record question is to protect them from getting more tickets if they were a habitual speeder, and if so then recommend a slower vehicle. Looking out for their best interest in that fashion would be a much better way to build rapport than to start with asking questions about their budget. Even if they still selected a faster vehicle, you would still be viewed as someone looking out for their best interest. To all of the car salesmen, and sales women reading this - you are very welcome. Proper questioning also eliminates objections from surprising you in later phases of your process. The more you find out in the greeting and the discovery, the smoother every other step will go.

In order to effectively discover that you have a product or service that a customer wants, the customer has to be very comfortable with you. You have to become one with the prospect, so you must be very alert and intuitive throughout the entire process, recognizing and addressing any resistance. After you greet the customer effectively, as described in the previous chapter, give an overview of the time they will spend with you, so they know what to expect and how long the entire process will be. During this time of the discussion it is very important that you are listening intently to pick up on what type of personality/personalities you are dealing with. This allows you to custom fit your delivery to fit their style of communication.

I recommend you ask them a question during this phase that allows you to find out what their past experience with your company was like. If they have never done any business with your company in particular, find out what their experience with the industry has been. If it has been great, find out what made it so nice, and making sure you deliver a similar experience is best, however, if it wasn't so wonderful, documenting the issue and addressing why it shouldn't happen again will help you gain early credibility. It is best that you discuss all objections up front so that when you begin presenting, they are able to truly listen to you. The best listening takes place when the customer is in a state of ease. Hidden turmoil clogs up the ear canals.

To discover correctly, your listening skills are very important. It might be a surprise to the novice salesperson/service professional, however, the fact is that the top producers are always the best listeners especially in the beginning of a face-to-face presentation. Remember that people usually only want to hear what is in it for them. Your entire goal is to position the experience for their benefit. In order to properly do that you cannot be the one speaking during the majority of this phase of the process. When your mastery of UNIVERSAL TALKING truly develops, the prospect ends up comfortably explaining to you how to help them by answering the well thought out questions you ask. Your main questions should be pre-planned to aim in a customized direction based upon the best strategy to help the customer. You will receive different responses from different customer types so notate the questions that give you the best responses, and then use them for future reference.

Another great way to discover is to listen to who answers the questions and how they answer. If I ask a couple how long they have been married and the wife looks at the husband as he looks away in a shy manner then she reluctantly answers, "twenty-two happy years," that tells me that she has the memory, she was hoping that her husband would have answered, she is proud of those twenty-two years, and that he has probably forgotten some other important memories in the past. These are little easy-to-overlook clues that can help you if you recognize them early in your discovery. If I ask that same question to a couple and the husband states after winking at his wife in a playful manner, "she has been trying to replace me since day one" and then hugs her, that tells me that they like joking around with each other, and that will be the style of communication I use with them.

Once you start to gain a true understanding of the client base you come in contact with daily, you will gain the art of being able to plant seeds during the discovery that should make the recommendation part of the process very simple. If done incorrectly the seeds you plant can cause more harm than help, so timing is very important. Remember, all steps must be genuinely delivered for maximum benefit to the customer. For instance, if I work in a furniture store and a couple comes in asking for a bedroom set with certain specification requirements, I can greet them and then plant a few seeds of a sale with a few statements. I might say, "That is a very wise selection, and we are finding it very hard to keep that bedroom set in stock because of the comfort and look associated with that brand. Were you just browsing or are you prepared to upgrade your quality of bedroom life sooner than later? If sooner I would like to make sure you are on the waiting list as early as possible to avoid any possible availability complications." The seeds planted in that early part of the meeting genuinely acknowledges their wisdom for being interested in that style, and the fact that it is hard to keep that style in stock, which decreases the chance of them wanting to come back *if* it's in stock. It also allows you to do a trial close, allowing you to determine if they are willing to take ownership of the product with a test question very early in the presentation.

To properly know what seeds to plant you have to truly understand the industry you are involved in, the average client's mindset in regards to the industry, and the economic condition of the area where you provide service. The most important reality that has to be understood is that in order to succeed consistently you have to constantly be growing in knowledge of your task at hand. If you really start getting better at understanding your process, the acceptance of the service by the client happens before the recommendation stage takes place.

Depending on the service you provide, the discovery will vary. Using the customer's style of communication to get your idea across, getting an idea of why they are considering the product/service/idea, how they will use the product/service/idea, and how long they plan on using it can give you an idea of how to custom fit the product to fit their particular needs. Compare the completed sales process to a custom-fitted suit on the body of your prospect. You will never skip a thorough discovery process again once you remember that you cannot get a suit tailored unless proper measurements are taken.

SUMMARY   You have learned that the greeting process described in Chapter 8 is primarily used to totally disarm the customer of all defenses so that you can discover the information that you'll need to know to help them. You are aware that in order to properly gain information correctly to custom fit the idea/service/product to their benefit you have to aggressively listen and recognize all signals that are given during the conversation. You have learned what planting seeds means, and how to use those seeds you plant to aid in the direction you would like your customer to go, effectively getting your point across without directly saying it. You are aware that your knowledge of your industry has to continuously grow so that you can properly prepare the correct questions to ask as you discover what will work best for your customer. You are aware that the discovery is critical in that it allows you to tailor the solution you are providing to the customer's exact fit.

Chapter 10

Company Credibility

If you know the true history of a holiday
it can bring much more meaning
to its celebration. KD

Y ou are the company. Whether you are a business owner, executive, representative, server or intern you represent a brand. It is imperative that you put the weight of the perception of the company on your back with your every move. When a customer mentions to others having been in your establishment, the way you treat them is what they remember and describe. The people who embrace this understanding always excel faster in life and gain more out of their daily interactions than those who do not.

I am a true believer that your prospect should know what the company has accomplished to demonstrate building value. One of the biggest mistakes I have seen people in sales make is assuming the prospect already knows the history of the company. As a UNIVERSAL TALKER, to prevent missing important value, make the extra effort to bring them up to date. In some cases, dependent upon the strategic questions you have asked in your discovery, company credibility may be a more detailed explanation with one prospect than with another, however, it is mandatory every single time. If your company is new, you should promote how you are going to provide future growth, and why there is a need for the company. This is done by simply displaying the track record of the company through a timeline which details critical moments that have contributed to the company's growth in general. One fundamental key before ever asking for business is to clearly state the forward movement of the company, and the reasons that drive that direction. The positive and progressive momentum of your company should contribute added security to the prospect wanting to start or maintain more of a relationship with your establishment. The first time I did a sales presentation and the customer told me how thankful he was because of what I'd covered, I began to realize in order to separate myself from the pack, I had to take care of mastering all of the little things for the customer's overall benefit.

To take this concept a step further, if a past, current, or future client comes into your establishment and they do not take advantage of the service offered due to your negligence, you have not only failed yourself but you have also failed the prospect. Vacations, cell phones, houses, gym memberships, jewelry, make-up, vehicles, clothes, child care, and the list goes on, are all services/products that can significantly enhance someone's life. If you have the ability to help deliver that experience, you need to understand the ways it could benefit their family. There should be no difference in how seriously you take your position in comparison to a Navy SEAL's assignment. When that Navy SEAL goes out on a mission, there cannot be mistakes. Mistakes cost lives when in a war zone and the importance of your job description should be held in that same regard. When I was in the Air Force I learned several lessons and one of the most important was learning that attention to detail is one of the critical traits you should have in all actions you participate in.

When you agree to undertake any job description it must be understood that the ripple you start has an effect on much more than just yourself. You are literally responsible for a chain of events that will happen or not happen because of you. Deactivating any thoughts associated with your job requirements that conflict with these steps are mandatory for you to separate from average performers. Regardless of your intentions when you decide to work for a company, it is a must that you fully commit to representing yourself as the company's biggest asset. As such, you should be proud of your company's accomplishments, and the people you talk to should be fully aware of them as well. Every position you hold in life should be looked at as training for the next position. By mastering your current level of expertise and knowledge of the company, you will become great at teaching it to others as you move up or if one day you are running your own organization. Whether you own or work for a company, your mindset should reflect a personal oath to yourself that you will do what's best for your organization. If the company you work for is reputable, the service you deliver should tie right in with the growth and timeline of the company and be a direct reflection of why they should do business with you today.

If an employer has to decide between six candidates for a position and all have similar qualifications, the applicant who researched the company's history and explains the culture and what it would mean to him to be employed there will have the highest chance of getting the job. A thorough company credibility explanation adds value to the candidate seeking employment. The same is true when a prospect is inquiring about doing business with your company. A simple rule in business that you can never go wrong by following is to always conduct the delivery of information as if you are on an interview.

SUMMARY You have learned that the entire view of the company you own or work for is placed on your back when you are delivering a customer experience. You have learned that building value in your company by giving the history of where you started and the direction you are going is a very important step in the process. You are now clear that a fundamental principle involved in asking for any participation is to explain the reasons why the product/idea/service is expanding. You have learned that in order to succeed and grow at your maximum ability with any product/service/idea, you have to deliver your presentation with the importance of a do or die mission. You have learned that all interactions in a business setting have to be undertaken with the detail that you would give at an interview for a position.

Chapter 11

The Recommendation Phase

*To become an excellent detective one
crucial step is being able to uncover all of the
motives behind the crime committed. KD*

The phase where you make a recommendation will vary depending on the nature of what idea/service/product that you present, however, there are fundamental principles that should be followed. Regardless of what goods and services are being provided there is certain information that must be gathered in order to properly recommend. The two biggest mistakes made in the sales environment are recommending options that are not suitable for the prospect, and making a recommendation without the prospect being in the correct mode to receive the suggestion. The emotions of the prospect before you recommend anything, is one of the major keys to whether your advice is accepted or not. Set up is crucial to your desired results in all steps taken throughout the entire process.

A very important part of the recommendation process is ensuring that you do not unintentionally cause your customer's defenses to rise. One of the quickest ways to get a prospect that you hardly know on the defense is by telling them what you think they should do based upon your opinion. You may have slightly lowered some of the tension through conversation, but usually they are just waiting for your fangs to come out which could happen if you fail to personalize the recommendation. The fundamental way to avoid that barrier is by remembering that almost all direction to them should be given through a third party story using the information gathered from the discovery.

A third party story allows you to explain an action to someone through a story that involves someone else's situation, instead of directly using the person or people you are talking to in the example. For instance, "Based off of the research you told me you did last night, it was a great choice to look in this area for your home because each of the families I have talked to in the past two years that purchased, also loved that view of the water from the back patio." That is much more impactful than "I think this view is perfect for you and your family based upon the specifications you asked for." You can also use third party stories to warn someone of a danger they should avoid. "The last two people I talked to said the gym is always busy during these hours so you are several steps ahead to pick this one here in midtown because you will have more space and comfort when you exercise. With your schedule, time is of the essence, so I will only sign you up for three training sessions this month instead of once per week okay?" Once you reach mastery level, your entire presentation is a mixture of emotionally triggering third party stories that make great points without causing any resistance at all.

You have to make suggestions accurately because you instantly lose credibility if what you recommend is not designed for their benefit. Another very important part of the recommendation process is the part that allows you to speak to your client as if the service that you are going to provide today should have already been taken advantage of a long time ago. Once done correctly the prospect starts to take ownership of the idea and you highly increase the chance of them taking advantage of the service/product today. If I missed the opportunity to get fifty percent off of a particular brand of tank tops that I loved because the sale ended two weeks ago, and in the store the salesperson gives me the chance to retroactively take advantage of it, I am going to move on it because I feel that I missed out. You achieve much better results when the client buys from you verses you selling to them.

The following statements will give you an example of how the verbiage would be if someone walked into 'KINJA ELECTRONICS' browsing for a Blue Ray player to replace their DVD player using the "this should have already been done" approach. "I commend you for having an appreciation for quality when it comes to how you view personal entertainment in your kingdom. Are you familiar with the history of the Blue Ray player? No? That answer makes sense and explains why you didn't get this system in your life years ago when they first launched. The major advantages are better image quality, better sound quality and special features with your menu options that are not available with the DVD player. What I am going to do for you once all your questions are answered and I get your price point, is see what your options are. Several models are on back order because of the high demand associated with this life enhancement."

In that example the key points covered were verbally acknowledging their wisdom for coming in, asking for their knowledge about the history of the product, stating features of the new system, making sure that the customer received full understanding that the items are rarely in stock, and most importantly expressing that these benefits should have already been in their world years ago.

Now that I have expressed the way to recommend, I have to give some insight on how to handle the client that does not readily accept your recommendation even though you custom fit it to their needs. In these scenarios there are a few possibilities that have caused the customer to go against the flow. For you to grow, self-accountability is required. No matter what the outcome, you must ask yourself what you could have done to net a better result. That is a much better habit to get into than the alternative, which is to point fingers. Pointing fingers takes self-analysis out of the equation, which results in less self-improvement.

Now back to the customer who all of a sudden resists your advice after you have, in your mind, given the best recommendation. You have to put yourself in their shoes. Maybe they either don't trust you, don't like your style of communication, don't agree that what you are saying will fully work the way you are describing it, or are not ready to move forward because it is just not that important to them. As you reflect on your prior steps, you should learn to recognize where you made your error, however, this is when negotiation skills come into play. This is the instant when the best communicators overcome and the rest wave good-bye as the prospect walks out of the door.

The first rule of thumb in becoming a great negotiator is complete self-control. The second is to always recognize that you understand the other person's point of view prior to addressing a way to get on common ground. When you react in a non-controlled fashion and show no understanding of how the prospect feels when you are the reason they feel that way, your results will hardly ever remain positive. If the client is on the defense, it is imperative that you realize how fragile their feelings are at that moment, and if you are not in a controlled state you will not be able to properly bring them back to ease. At the critical point when a customer is being resistant, the only way to bring them back is with proper strategic questioning which can only occur if you are in a state of productivity. Calmness always presents a feeling of confidence that helps the emotion in the room sway in your favor during the negotiations for two main reasons. First, your thoughts are much more creative, leading you to ask better questions. Second, your calm approach will always bring them into a more receptive state. Body language is also important during this process so stay leaned back in a very non-aggressive posture as you get them back on track.

As you maneuver through this process one great method of getting the prospects back into the direction that you'd like is to end all of the points you make with a question that draws a yes out of them. For instance, "I am very happy that you are finally seeing the benefit of how this will work for you and your family. Since having a lower payment was your greater focus, putting the least amount down within your budget that would have the best effect on lowering your payment would be best for you correct? And since the minivan is much more spacious than the jeep, if I can use these rebates to lower your family's out-of-pocket expenses more than what I originally informed you, any extra savings would help out, correct? "

The first time that you impose your calm yet powerful will to turn that client around, you must take a moment and write down exactly what took place and reflect on it. Here are a few of the questions that must be answered after the process:

- How can I properly get my future clients more comfortable to draw out their true objections earlier?
- What could I have done to smoothly transition without any resistance?

- During the negotiation process what did I say to get my desired response from them?

The goal is to slowly but surely put together a resistance proof delivery, however mastering how to transition through turbulence has to also be focused on, as well. As you master the process you will encounter less resistance and the results you desire should occur easier and more often as you smoothly transition through each phase of your presentation. Practice makes perfect, so as you go forward in your craft of meeting clients, and aiming to help one hundred percent of those you come in contact with, you will see progress in your production.

SUMMARY You have learned that before you recommend any idea/service/product to a customer, the customer has to be completely comfortable. You have learned that third party stories are a very effective way to make strong points without causing defenses to rise. You have learned that it is better for someone to buy into the idea/service/product instead of you having to sell it, by explaining that it is something that should have already been done. You have learned that getting the customer to say yes to small questions is a great way to increase reception to the sale. You are clear that self-control and remaining calm are two of the most important parts of the negotiation process.

Chapter 12

The Closing of the Sale

*The architect who designs a home
without any doors does not worry about them
ever being closed. Planning is everything. KD*

The closing of the sale is the part of the sales process where the deal is completely sealed and the prospect takes full ownership of the idea/service/product that you have shown will benefit their life. This part of your process has to be in mind before you even meet the prospect, however, it cannot hinder you from following the previous steps of the process. That is, you have to go into the interaction expecting a positive outcome at all times, but you cannot put the cart before the horse.

I want you to compare the closing of the sale to the starting of a car. In order for the key to turn and cause the vehicle to start, there are a series of very important mechanical processes that take place to make that action occur. If the steps prior to the close are not in perfect alignment "the car" to your sale will not start, and it is just that simple. Once the steps prior to the close are handled with precision it is very simple to seal the deal in personal or business transactions. If you focus on the means, the ends shall come. That principle is part of every positive result that you are looking for in life. All consistently successful people you have ever known took several thousands of hours of practice steps before their victories came consistently. The best part of being in the sales/service industry is that you actually get a chance to win every single time you interact with the customer. The mindset that comes with it turns you into a much better person if you allow it to, whether you get the sale or not. The additional strength to your character that comes with this process is priceless and should not be taken lightly. If you embrace what you just read you will look at the entire sales process in a brand new light.

With the car analogy in mind, you can now understand that if you encounter any sales scenario where the close is the toughest part of the process, your previous steps are totally responsible for those results. A car simply starts when you turn the key if it is in the correct condition, and that is the same way the close should occur if the greeting, discovery, company credibility and recommendation goes the way it should to ultimately benefit the prospect. The closing should actually be the easiest part because they should by this time already have taken acceptance that this solution is what they need due to the previous steps being completed successfully. The best part about the experience is that you can usually track what part of your process was out of line and simply correct it going forward if the close does not happen as easily as I suggest. Documentation is an excellent way to keep a progress report on what your best steps were on a daily basis. Self-reflection can turn anyone into a better person regardless of what you are attempting to improve in your life.

The absolute worst thing you could do is to get used to not closing the deal. Accepting defeat is suicidal in my eyes, especially when you have the ability to control your future interactions, which is the great part about life. Statements like "Nobody could have sold them" or "That customer was just broke" or "It is just not the right time for them" are all backed by a mindset of complacency in your possible abilities. In all three statements I see an area of improvement for the person that made it. Your personality wasn't versatile enough with the first statement, you didn't create the need and value with the second, and the urgency for the need of the idea/service/product was not delivered, in the third. Your close percentages are increased by changing your character into a constantly growing machine. Every living being can be persuaded, as opposed to thinking of all the other possibilities. I would rather explore what I could have done to help that client see the benefit. More growth comes with the "What could I have done better?" approach than the "I did all that I could do" approach.

In order to be a success in life and to truly become a consistent dominator in sales, you must be self-reliant. This characteristic ensures that you are fully responsible for your well-being in life and in sales it puts the responsibility of your steps being handled on your back. In most sales environments the beginner is trained to do the introductory steps and then after the prospect seems ready to go forward they bring the closer in to finish the sales process. I have been blessed to be in the top five percent of the industry of face to face sales for eleven of the twelve years that I have been involved and the people that made the choice to let that closer take responsibility for closing their sales every time have been severely handicapped. The path of least resistance is the most commonly traveled road to mediocrity. Based upon the principles that I have studied in life my future is totally under my control and no one else's.

I was blessed to work with a young man by the name of Sean Vaughn who said something in a team meeting that will stick with me for life. It went something like this: "As an adult you have to go to the store, pick out the food you would like to eat, and then bring it home and cook it to eat to nourish your body. Babies and young children need you to pick out their food and prepare it for them to survive. If you are an adult there is no way that you should ever put the responsibility of your survival into the hands of someone else." Those words universally apply to several areas in one's life. He was giving feedback in regards to people who were starting to get dependent on others to close their business, which he noticed lowered their expectation of what they were capable of. Going back eons ago, the principles of taking care of self and family were instilled into all living creatures in order for them to survive. Why is it that in life and in so many sales industries it seems as if this way of thinking is outdated? The answer to that will explain why only few in life and in sales excel and reach the potential they are truly capable of.

Throughout life and your career you should seek strategic assistance to help your overall steps as you aim to make yourself stronger. Using someone to help you close your deals is great in the beginning to help improve your technique. Assistance should be viewed as something temporary and not as a permanent crutch. The Master Closer does involve others however they are involved by choice, not by need. There have been several times in my career where I have brought someone in as a third party to document the information that the customer was not aware of. Those times were for positioning and not by any form, a need. My thoughts have always been that I had better make myself capable of doing everything just in case for reasons out of my control I had no one to assist. In the process, you use more brain power which in turn always broadens your tolerance level for any difficulties. Delegation is great to get more accomplished, however, it is not a substitute for increasing your skill set. The team will be much more prosperous if all members are fully independent contributors to the interdependence of the entire operation.

I am a product of tough love, and I do realize not everyone has had that type of experience. My message on the closing of the sale may be slightly different than what you have heard from others, however, I must explain why the message may be different. My knowledge and insight has been derived by continuous self-development and constant growth from other successful individuals. There has never been a ceiling in place to limit me on how high I can go and there never will be. Remove any limits that have been placed on your abilities, as well. Trial and error from actually selling for a living for a total of twelve years (4,380 days), at an average of six hours a day (26, 280 hours) has provided me with proven success principles that have steadily increased my results year after year. To perform at a top level, you are going to have to be different from the normal people that float around daily just existing in their chosen craft while becoming dependent on others. In every area of your life it always pays to be exceptional and self-reliant.

Now as we get detailed into the process of sealing your deal, I want to explore how to give the options that are all beneficial to the client in the end. In my experience the choice close has worked to the customer's benefit the most. I have fully accepted that road and have traveled it ever since. The benefit that I was taught in using the choice close is to give options so that the client can choose what is best for him instead of only giving one option. Giving one option leaves a greater chance of the customer being backed in a corner which I personally do not like. Usually the choice close includes two to three options at most that will each benefit the customer in different ways. Regardless of what he chooses, we all win when he leaves happy that he made a great decision, and you leave happy because you provided great service.

If there is reluctance for any reason, a brief recap is in order. In the end the client may fear change. This is natural so stay calm in your posture and tone, then simply remind him of the situation that led to that point. Reiterate why he needs the solution based off of the information he provided you in the discovery and the long term benefit to his forward progression that was already agreed upon during the company credibility. Doing so should overcome the concern. If he does not get back on track at that point, understand there are several other reasons customers can continuously be resistant. Those reasons can derive from a non-genuine greeting causing him to just go along with you versus truly becoming engaged, a poorly conducted discovery that didn't give you true insight on how the purchase of your product or service can be to his benefit, or a recommendation that he sees no benefit in. Regardless of the reason, realize that the resistance ultimately means you have some steps to work on. The best part about it is that whatever the reason for resistance you can link it to a step in your process, then reflect and strategize on how to improve upon that step. Tracking and pinpointing that step will simply take personal initiative on your part.

Once the client chooses an option, the first step of the close is complete. The second step is to ask a question that allows the customer to explain in his own words why that choice is the best option for him, and allow him to elaborate. This allows you to learn what emotions were triggered for future presentations. The third step is to get a To-Do List set up that builds a three to twelve month timeline of follow-up tasks for the customer to keep you in the loop as he enjoys the idea/service/product. The fourth step is to get a list of referrals from him in order to give his close family/friends/other businesses the ability to take advantage of your professional assistance.

The fifth step is to trade personal contact information because from this point on, the client should feel free to reach out to you about the product/service/idea in the future. The sixth and final step includes a follow up call within a day or two just for any questions that may have arisen since the deal was sealed.

The people who believe that the close is a one-step motion are the ones that have a higher return rate than those with a closing system. A store can sell one million items, but if fifty percent of the merchandise is returned the net result is a lot of additional work completed for half the profit. A profitable business thrives because of its solid and continuous repeat customers, and in sales/service/life you are considered a store within yourself.

The answers will always present themselves
if you are strong enough to look at yourself
as the problem. KD

SUMMARY You have learned that contrary to what you have ever heard, the close should be the simplest part of the sales process once the greeting, discovery, company credibility, and recommendation steps have been done correctly. You have learned that if your results are not what you intend, constant self-analysis is the only way to ensure that you deliver better results going forward, versus making excuses. You have learned that regardless of the system, you will aggressively strive to become self-reliant in all tasks to ensure you do not get dependent on anyone or anything to ensure your survival in the workplace or in life. You have learned that when you give two to three options when it comes to a product or service, you allow the customer to take control and pick which one is best for them. You have realized that it is best to create a closing system to properly serve the customer, which helps your overall retention and business model.

Chapter 13

Successful Living Comes With Commitment

*In every minute of your life there is a lesson
to be learned, and during this school season
you cannot go on lunch break. KD*

Thank you for reading the first of many forms of self-development that I am going to contribute to this world. My main goal has been accomplished if my thoughts have combined with yours to create a broader outlook on the future steps that you will take in life. As you travel this never-ending road to make yourself a better person, you must stay focused because the temptation to become mediocre sometimes may block your vision.

You can spend energy to improve your life, or to take actions that are not helpful to yourself and others. Because of the times that we are facing it is more important than ever that we get our minds in the right place. When you start to take the self-development route, realize that unfortunately some of your family and friends may not be ready to come with you. Once you expose them to your journey and they resist be careful that your intent to help is not wasted on unresponsive people. I want the best for the world but everyone is not ready to become great.

The principles to become an effective communicator are consistent with being a productive person, so do not limit the lessons. This book was written by a professional sales-person, however, the principles will help any person who is willing to grow regardless of their place in life. Aiming for mastery in each of your daily tasks is a choice that most do not make, and your lifestyle of today will always be a reflection of your previous decisions. Be better than you were yesterday and help someone else do the same.

I have a few action plan recommendations that helped me when I was first exposed to a more accountable way of living. Take a moment and reflect on the different chapters of your life that brought you to where you are today and number them. For instance, chapter one could be childhood, chapter two could be high-school and so forth. Write down the important mistakes you made and in what areas you excelled during your personal and business matters and why. Once you target the mistakes, go back through your chapters to see where the trait that caused that mistake originated and then simply correct that behavior. This is where the library, self-development and research should be implemented. The best part about figuring out where it originated is that it will make it much easier to correct.

The next action that has truly helped me, which I gained from reading *The 7 Habits of Highly Effective People,* by Stephen Covey is starting and maintaining a daily journal. Your new ideas, lessons learned, experiences and life story in general needs to be documented. Some of the benefits are that your memory is trained by the brief recap at the end of each evening, you learn more about your life from looking at it from an objective stand point versus subjective, and it allows a great way for your current/future children/family members to gain wisdom down the road from certain points in your growth.

The last action that I am going to recommend is that you reread any book geared toward self-help including this one at least four times. I am living proof that great self-development is just like a movie with six to seven sub plots, that you've watched more than once or twice. Every time you watch it, you notice or understand something that you didn't fully catch the first time. I have read *Rich Dad Poor Dad* at least five times and took something new away each session. It also will reaffirm what you learned from the first few times, which only makes it better for you in the long run.

In closing I am going to make another commitment to you and this world. For every 10,000 sold copies of this work, one of the purchasers will be randomly selected and given $5000 in cash. Each selected recipient will also be able to choose a charity of his or her choice, to which my company, KD Excellence Consulting will publicly donate another $5000 on the behalf of that recipient. The name of the success drive is **10 for Every 10**. I would like to be one of the first authors to automatically give to charity, provide mental wealth, and distribute personal financial blessings as sales of this book grow. As this plan pays out hundreds of thousands and maybe even millions to the beneficiaries of the UNIVERSAL TALK LAWS please take note and be proud to be a part of history.

To register for the **10 for Every 10** success drive, just simply e-mail your name, receipt number, how you discovered this book along with any of your testimonials in regards to the content, best day and evening telephone numbers, and the charity that you would donate to if you were to be selected as a winner and why. This information can be emailed to kdixon@kinjadixon.com. As the book breaks through each level of growth, the recipients selected will be personally contacted and emailed with instructions on how to claim the proceeds for themselves and for the designated charity. Do not forget to register. Each book owner, once registered will permanently have a chance at winning, so if you purchase a few for your family or friends, decide whose name will be sent on behalf of each book with the registry prior to your entry for the drive.

For instance, one of my close friends told me his plans of buying 400 copies of UNIVERSAL TALK LAWS for his entire organization that he manages. He admits that his style of managing did not include much personal development and his plan is to implement more of a purpose driven environment so that everyone could benefit more in and out of the office. He plans on giving them away as gifts so each of the recipients can gain from the guidance and also register their book for the **10 for Every 10** success drive under each of their names, however, if he wanted he could register each book under his name giving him 400 permanant chances at being selected as an alternative option.

New life begins only when you have outgrown the space that your current life has created. KD

Highlights from UNIVERSAL TALK LAWS

- When I did research to help motivate my team I learned that being able to properly communicate is a similar trait in all successful people.

- Each day is a gift and you should be eager to open up your daily present.

- Only focus on what you can control to avoid your emotional cup from overflowing with the wrong emotion.

- Always think in the most positive manner to progress in life, especially during tough times.

- Life will always throw you unexpected situations, however, you can surely know that there are ways to deal with all adversity to make you a better person afterward.

- Luck is when massive preparation meets opportunity.

- The quicker you realize how important the art of communication is to your life progression, the faster you will advance.

- You can be content with what you have but you should never be content with who you are as a person. Growth should be constant.

- You are the only certified mechanic that can truly work on your mental car, and where you end up on a daily basis is totally dependent on how well your work is continuously done with it.

- Every position that you hold in life should be viewed as training for your next position.

- Accepting defeat is suicidal, especially when you have the ability to control your future interactions which is the great part about life.

- The path of least resistance is the most commonly traveled road to mediocrity.

- There has never been a ceiling in place to limit how high I can go and there never will be. Remove any limits that have been placed on your abilities as well.

For further self-development I recommend:

Think and Grow Rich by Napoleon Hill
Outiers by Malcom Gladwell
Unlimited Power by Anthony Robbins
Compound Effect by Darren Hardy
The Alchemist by Paulo Coelho
Rich Dad, Poor Dad by Robert Kiyosaki
5 Love Languages by Gary Chapman
7 Habits of Highly Effective People by Stephen Covey
Rough Guide to Psychology by Dr. Christian Jarrett
Expect To Win by John Mason
The Power of the Subconscious Mind by Joseph Murphy
The Science of Getting Rich by Wallace D. Wattles
As a Man Thinketh by James Allen
The Magic of Believing by Claude M. Bristol

These are some of the books that enhanced my view over the years, and I consistently aim to read at least one new book per month. This world is filled with knowledge in all forms so take advantage of the minutes that form days that lead to your current and future status. For my people on the go, audiobooks are a great way to gain insight while you travel throughout your day handling any of your daily duties. For every one that makes an excuse, another makes a way.

More Acknowledgments

There can never be too much gratitude. Due to my belief that there can be positivity gained from each life interaction, regardless of the circumstance, I would like to name a few people that during my life have contributed to my foundation. I will be forever grateful for what I have learned through each of these individuals. I encourage each reader to focus on living a life that adds motivation to someone else in the same fashion.

Esther Adeoye, Keith Aveyard, Michael Badlam Jr., Michael Badlam, Travis Bary, Andre Bentley, Dr. A.R. Bernard, John Bird, T.A. Bragg, Kevin Brown, Brendon Buirski, Maria Capocelli, Cydni Clay, Insana Collins, Neil Conway, Shauntae Covington, Julianne Couch, Jessica Cuff, Robert Cuff Sr., Brian Decker, Alcedric Dixon, Robert Dixon, Willie Dixon, Ben Douglas, Brad Fox, Morrell Gaines, Dwayne Govain, Kevin Gray, Franz Hanning, Clifton Hargett, Travis Harris, Calvin Harris, Michael Hecht, Bill Henderson, French Hicks, Anita Howell, Dave Hubbard, Christy Humphrey, Sherry Jean, Monique Johnson, Rick Jones, Elam King, Warren Knight, Beverly Knight, Latoya Leary, Leslie Lee, Nikkia Lewis, Kohly, Jay Manselle, Maria Margenot, Lee Mcdowell, Caprice Mclarin, Curtis Mclarin, Shelly Miles, Barbara Moore, Eric Morace, Jeff Myers, Moses Newsome, Loren Nester, Phu Nguyen, Mike Odwyer, Mr. P, Robert Parker, Alexis Perkins, Aaron Piotroski, P.J. Priester, Brittany Reed, Makeda Richardson, Ramon Rodriguez, Claudia Rogosch, Henry Rush, Mark Schilling, Mike Schott, Catherine Sharpe, Derek Sherman, Robert Shepard,

Brian Smalls, Lerrod Smalls, Dr. C.L. Spells, Kevin Sutton, Carol Swayne, Onella Taitt, Derek Taylor, Thomas Thompson, Earlene Thorpe, Steve Vaught, Janice Washington, Diane Watson, Nidra Webster, Edward Wilkins, Tina Wilkins, Klaleh York, and Mike Zanda.